A TREASURY
OF AL-GHAZALI

THE TREASURY SERIES IN
ISLAMIC THOUGHT AND CIVILISATION

I. *A Treasury of Ḥadīth*, Ibn Daqīq al-ʿĪd

II. *A Treasury of al-Ghazālī*, Mustafa Abu Sway

III. *A Treasury of Sacred Maxims*, Shahrul Hussain

IV. *A Treasury of Ibn Taymiyyah*, Mustapha Sheikh

V. *A Treasury of Rūmī*, Muhammad Isa Waley

VI. *A Treasury of Iqbal*, Abdur Rashid Siddiqui
(Forthcoming)

VII. *A Treasury of ʿĀ'ishah*, Sofia Rehman
(Forthcoming)

Mustafa Abu Sway

❧ ❧ ❧

كنوز من الغزالي
A TREASURY OF
AL-GHAZALI

*A Companion for the
Untethered Soul*

KUBE
PUBLISHING

A man came to the Messenger of Allah ﷺ, and asked: 'O Messenger of Allah! Who is entitled among the people to the best of my companionship? He answered: Your mother He asked [again]: Then who? He answered: Your mother He asked [for the third time]: Then who? He answered: Your mother He asked [one last time]: Then who? He answered: Then your father'
(Al-Bukhārī and Muslim)

THIS BOOK IS DEDICATED ACCORDINGLY;
THREE TIMES TO MY LATE MOTHER, AND
ONCE TO MY FATHER

*A Treasury of al-Ghazālī: A Companion
for the Untethered Soul*

First published in England by
Kube Publishing Ltd
Markfield Conference Centre
Ratby Lane, Markfield
Leicestershire LE67 9SY
United Kingdom

TEL +44 (0)1530 249230
FAX +44 (0)1530 249656
WEBSITE www.kubepublishing.com
EMAIL info@kubepublishing.com

CIP data for this book is available from the British Library.

ISBN 978-1-84774-081-6 casebound
ISBN 978-1-84774-116-5 ebook

Cover design Inspiral Design
Book design Imtiaze Ahmed
Arabic & English typesetting nqaddoura@hotmail.com
Printed by Elma Basim, Turkey

Contents

{CEND} {CEND} {CEND}

Transliteration Table   VIII

Acknowledgments   IX

Introduction   1

1   Education with the Right Intention   6
2   Are You in the Wrong Business?   9
3   Seek Felicity   12
4   Introspection   15
5   Do Your Good Deeds Outnumber
     Your Bad Ones?   18
6   The Greatest Pleasure of All   22
7   Deconstructing Greek Metaphysics   25
8   Do not Eat Your Path to Heaven   29
9   The Merits of Marriage   33
10 Striving Beyond Justice   36
11 Degrees of Piety   39
12 The Fruit of Divine Love   42
13 Travelling   46
14 Listening to Songs   50
15 Enjoining Good and Forbidding Evil   53
16 Behaviour is the Mirror of the Heart   57
17 Flames of Repentance   60
18 Patience in Avoiding Sin   63
19 True Grace   67

20 A Plantation for the Hereafter 70
21 Shamefully Busy 74
22 Sins as True Veils 77
23 Occasionalism (Allah is the Cause
     of all Events) 81
24 Love is the Renewed Imperative 84
25 On Knowledge, Action and Sincerity 88
26 There Are Absolutely No Secrets 91
27 Thinking and Having a Preference
     for the Eternal 94
28 Remembering Death 98
29 Knowledge vs. Gold and Silver 102
30 Presenting Faith to Children 106
31 External Cleansing and Internal
     Purification 110
32 Deconstructing Distractions 113
33 Fasting Has Three Degrees 117
34 Liberation from Attachments 121
35 Involvement of the Tongue, Intellect and
     Heart in Reciting the Holy Qur'ān 125
36 Knowing Allah Is a Matter of the Heart 128
37 Inculcating Beautiful Personal Traits 132
38 Excessive Appetite for Food Unleashes
     Destructive Forces 135
39 Healing the Love for Status 139
40 Revolting Against Powerful
     Unjust Rulers 142

References 145
Index 147

Transliteration Table

Arabic Consonants

Initial, unexpressed medial and final: ء '

ا	a	د	d	ض	ḍ	ك	k
ب	b	ذ	dh	ط	ṭ	ل	l
ت	t	ر	r	ظ	ẓ	م	m
ث	th	ز	z	ع	'	ن	n
ج	j	س	s	غ	gh	هـ	h
ح	ḥ	ش	sh	ف	f	و	w
خ	kh	ص	ṣ	ق	q	ي	y

with a *shaddah*, both medial and final consonants are doubled.

Vowels, diphthongs, etc.

| Short: | ＿ a | ＿ i | ＿ u |
| Long: | ＿ا ā | ＿ي ī | ＿و ū |

| Diphthongs: | ＿وَ aw |
| | ＿ىَ ay |

Acknowledgments

*P*raise be to Him, who made it possible for this work to be, availing me and numerous others to contribute effort, in various degrees and manners, so that finally *A Treasury of al-Ghazālī* became a reality!

I would like to express my deep gratitude to the editors and managers at Kube Publishing for this wonderful opportunity to share Imam Al-Ghazālī's wisdom with a wider public, but mostly for the encouragement and patience. For this I will be ever grateful.

Thank you Haris Ahmad, without your direct support this book would not have come to light!

There are many scholars who, over a long period of time, edited and published Imām al-Ghazālī's works in various forms, in Arabic and other languages, publishers who realized the importance of serving the need for studies on al-Ghazālī, educational institutions in the East and the West who celebrate the heritage of Ḥujjat al-Islām, and very important intellectual and public figures who have the vision and work diligently to revive the wisdom, methodology and spiritual path of Imām al-Ghazālī. I am indebted to all of them. May this work be an extension of their good deeds.

A special thank you note to Ms. Kifah 'Ilayyan from the Colleges of Islamic Studies at Al-Quds University, for her help with typing the Arabic text.

Introduction

✤ ✤ ✤

*I*mām al-Ghazālī (450–505 AH/1058–1111 CE) of Tus, Khorasan, occupies a unique place in human history. Almost all of humanity today aspires to achieve what he abandoned in a moment of genuine transformation. By subscribing to the Sufi mystical path, he renounced the material world. He believed he had to 'shun fame, money and run away from obstacles' that prevented him from achieving indubitable knowledge. This spiritual crisis took place at the peak of his career at the Niẓāmiyyah College of Baghdad, a position that won him 'prestige, wealth and respect that even princes, kings and viziers could no match." (al-Zabīdī, *Ithāf al-Sādah al-Muttaqīn*, vol. I, p. 7)

His inward struggle was vividly described in *al-Munqidh min al-Ḍalāl*, where he stated:

> For nearly six months beginning from Rajab, 488 AH (July, 1095), I was continuously tossed between the attractions of worldly desires and the impulses towards eternal life. In that month the matter ceased to be one of choice and became one of compulsion. [Allah] caused my tongue to dry up so that I was prevented

from lecturing. One particular day I made an effort to lecture in order to gratify the hearts of my students, but my tongue would not utter a single word, nor could I accomplish anything at all.

His health declined and his physicians gave up on him, for they realised it was not a physical ailment that was wrong with him. At this stage, he 'sought refuge with Allah who made it easy for his heart to turn away from position and wealth, from children and friends.' (Hyman and Walsh, *Philosophy in the Middle Ages*, pp. 277–278)

And that is exactly what al-Ghazālī did! He left his job, distributed his wealth, except for the very little that he kept for the needs of his family. And in order to give up his power and fame, he left Baghdad to lands where he was not known. He lived incognito in Damascus, Jerusalem, and visited Hebron, Makkah and Madīnah. It took him eleven years before heading back home.

Al-Ghazālī carved a niche for himself in the world of Islamic thought. He was the scholar par excellence in the Islamic world, with hundreds of scholars attending his lectures at the Niẓāmiyyah school of Baghdad between 484 AH/1091 CE and 488 AH/1095 CE (cf. al-Subkī, *Ṭabaqāt al-Shāfiᶜiyyah al-Kubrā*, vol. VI, p. 197). His scholarly works in jurisprudence, theology, philosophy, education and Islamic spirituality continue to enrich academic discourse on the Islamic worldview. He became known as the 'Proof of Islam' (*Ḥujjat al-Islām*) for his role in defending Islam, especially against internal sectarian trends.

Imām al-Ghazālī's magnum opus, *Iḥyā' ʿUlūm al-Dīn* (*The Revival of the Religious Sciences*) continues to be celebrated for its ability to infuse spirituality into law (*fiqh*). The books of Islamic law are typically technical and dry. The traditional works of jurisprudence do not capture the Arabic etymological meaning of *fiqh* in the Holy Qur'ān and the Prophetic Sunnah. It denotes understanding the totality of the Islamic worldview, with spirituality at its core.

Imām al-Ghazālī's autobiographical work, *Al-Munqidh min al-Ḍalāl*, reflects an inquisitive mind that goes back to the days of his early childhood, and a fascination with indubitable knowledge and truth throughout his life. But it is his spiritual curiosity and captivating knowledge of the intimate affairs of the heart that constitute an exceptional source for all seekers of the meaning of life. He stated at the beginning of *al-Munqidh*: 'The thirst for grasping the real meaning of things was indeed my habit and wont from my early years and in the prime of my life. It was an instinctive, natural disposition placed in my makeup by Allah Most High, not something due to my own choosing and contriving. As a result, the fetters of servile conformism fell away from me and inherited beliefs lost their hold on me when I was quite young.'

Al-Ghazālī's works travelled far and wide. Some of them were translated into Latin within a very short period after his death. Reflecting the influence of al-Ghazālī on the Latin world, Manuel Alonso listed forty-four medieval philosophers and theologians who made reference to al-Ghazālī. These included Thomas Aquinas who referred to *Maqāṣid Al-Falāsifah* thirty-one times. (Al-Andalus, XXIII)

This book, *A Treasury of al-Ghazālī*, is an attempt to capture the essence of Imām al-Ghazālī's corpus of writings. He was prolific, leaving to posterity seventy-three books and treatises, which made choosing the forty maxims a challenging task because of the sheer number of possibilities available at hand.

Imām al-Ghazālī, like all Sufis, had an appreciation for 'taste' as experiential knowledge, not as sensory perception. After studying, teaching and writing about al-Ghazālī for more than three decades, I have developed a 'taste' for his ethos. He was an outstanding scholar of the Shāfiʿī school of jurisprudence, an Ashʿarite theologian and a Sufi. His story is that of returning to Allah, of having the right relationship with this world in preparation for the Hereafter, of abandoning bad personal traits and of inculcating good ones. The heart is at the centre of this story and it is the cornerstone of ethics and morality, but most crucially it is the single most important medium to understand and connect with the Divine.

The actual choice of these forty selections is reductionist at best; it cannot encompass all of al-Ghazālī's ideas and concerns, but they can definitely provide a 'taste' of his intellectual and spiritual message. It is hoped that *A Treasury of al-Ghazālī* will motivate the readers to further their studies of this great scholar and intellectual and read at least some of his works.

Today, there is a renewed interest in al-Ghazālī, for spiritual renewal and for academic reasons as well. The Integral Chair for the Study of Imām al-Ghazālī's Work at the Al-Aqsa Mosque and Al-Quds University (HM King Abdullah II Endowment); programmes at Cambridge Muslim College, UK; retreats during Ramadan at the Alqueria de Rosales in Spain; a Conference at Zaytuna College in Berkeley, USA; the annual Imām Al-Ghazālī lecture at Elmhurst College, USA, are but some of the manifestations of this renewed interest and spiritual revival.

I would like to end this introduction with one of al-Ghazālī's insights that there are more sciences within reach of human beings, he said: 'It appeared to me through clear insight and beyond doubt that man is capable of acquiring several sciences that are still latent and not existent.' (*Jawāhir al-Qur'ān*, p. 28)

A Treasury of Al-Ghazālī offers humanity one extra drink to quench its thirsty heart.

Written in the last occupied holy city in the twenty first century.

Mustafa Abu Sway

I

Education with the Right Intention

أَيُّهَا الوَلَد: كَمْ مِنْ لَيَالٍ أَحْيَيْتَهَا بِتِكْرَارِ العِلْمِ وَمُطَالَعَةِ الْكُتُبِ وَحَرَّمْتَ عَلَى نَفْسِكِ النَّوْمَ، لَا أَعْلَمُ مَا كَانَ الْبَاعِثُ فِيهِ! إِنْ كَانَ نَيْلُ عَرَضَ الدُّنْيَا وَجَذْبُ حُطَامِهَا وَتَحْصِيلُ مَنَاصِبِهَا وَالْمُبَاهَاةُ عَلَى الأَقْرَانِ وَالأَمْثَالِ فَوَيْلٌ لَكَ ثُمَّ وَيْلٌ لَكَ. وَإِنْ كَانَ قَصْدُكَ فِيهِ إِحْيَاءُ شَرِيعَةِ النَّبِيِّ صَلَّى اللهُ عَلَيْهِ وَسَلَّمَ وَتَهْذِيبُ أَخْلَاقِكَ وَكَسْرُ النَّفْسِ الأَمَّارَةِ بِالسُّوءِ فَطُوبَى لَكَ ثُمَّ طُوبَى لَكَ.[1]

O Son! How many nights have you stayed awake revising and memorising knowledge and poring over books, denying yourself sleep? I do not know what was the purpose of all this. If it was for the purpose of attaining worldly ends, securing its vanities and acquiring position and bragging before your peers, then woe

---

1. Al-Ghazālī, *Majmūᶜat Rasāʾil al-Imām al-Ghazālī*. Beirut: Dār al-Kutub al-ᶜIlmiyyah, 1986, pp.154–155.

to you! And again woe to you! But if your purpose for doing so was reviving the Sacred Law of the Prophet, may Allah bless him and grant him peace, refining your character and breaking the soul that commands to evil, then blessed are you! And again blessed are you!*

*I*n *Ayyuhā al-Walad* (*Dear Beloved Son!*), Imām al-Ghazālī responded to the request of one of his students, who obviously spent years seeking knowledge, for further advice as to what knowledge is beneficial in the light of the Hereafter.

This request, while it was about seeking deeper insight into advantageous knowledge in the Hereafter, may be applied to all human activity. What is done for the sake of Allah earns one reward and what is done for worldly motives ends right here at best, but could land one in an unfavourable position in the Afterlife, and there is nothing worse!

Seeking fame, position and material wealth as ends in themselves is detrimental to the soul, but this is exactly what people have sought throughout history. Islam is not against material gain if it is lawful, and if one spends lawfully, without being stingy or a spendthrift, and pays the alms, which renders wealth pure. Indeed, Islam is not against obtaining lawful and lawfully-earned wealth. Wholesome income sought from lawful sources, for

---

* Al-Ghazālī, *Ayyuhā al-Walad*, trans. by G.H. Scherer. Beirut: The American Press, 1932, p. 57.

the right purpose, is good for the individual and the community for it allows one to carry out different social responsibilities. Suffice to know that there were wealthy Prophetic Companions, including ʿUthmān ibn ʿAffān, the third Rightly-guided Caliph, and ʿAbd al-Raḥmān ibn ʿAwf. Many Prophetic Companions donated substantial amounts of their money or property for the sake of public good.

As for fame, if it comes as a result of civic engagement, scientific achievement, championing humanitarian causes or any other good deed for the welfare of society or humanity at large, without translating this fame into pretentious behaviour, then it is a good thing because it can be utilised to further whatever project one has embarked upon. Service to all, Muslim and non-Muslim, is the key to success. Muslims are invited to contribute towards eliminating illiteracy, providing fresh water and sanitation, and fighting disease and poverty everywhere.

Yet, one should be wary of the potential negative impact of fame on the heart. Positions of responsibility, such as holding public office, should undoubtedly be filled. But in that case one has to remember that one is a public servant, and that the relationship with the public is horizontal, not vertical. One is on the same level as that of the people one serves, not higher than them. There is a problem if one is not the right person for the job, or does not have the necessary skills. There is a more serious problem if one is seeking a position of responsibility for egotistic reasons, a hunger for power, as a means to unlawful gains or to inflict harm on others!

2

Are You in the Wrong Business?

فَاعْلَمْ أَيُّهَا الْحَرِيصُ الْمُقْبِلُ عَلَى اقْتِبَاسِ الْعِلْمِ الْمُظْهِرِ مِنْ
نَفْسِهِ صِدْقَ الرَّغْبَةِ وَفَرْطَ التَّعَطُّشِ إِلَيْهِ أَنَّكَ إِنْ كُنْتَ
تَقْصِدُ بِطَلَبِ الْعِلْمِ الْمُنَافَسَةَ وَالْمُبَاهَاةَ وَالتَّقَدُّمَ عَلَى الأَقْرَانِ
وَاسْتِمَالَةَ وُجُوهِ النَّاسِ إِلَيْكَ وَجَمْعَ حُطَامِ الدُّنْيَا فَأَنْتَ
سَاعٍ فِي هَدْمِ دِينِكَ وَهَلْكِ نَفْسِكَ وَبَيْعِ آخِرَتِكَ بِدُنْيَاكَ
فَصَفْقَتُكَ خَاسِرَةٌ وَتِجَارَتُكَ بَائِرَةٌ وَمُعَلِّمُكَ مُعِينٌ
لَكَ عَلَى عِصْيَانِكَ وَشَرِيكٌ لَكَ فِي خُسْرَانِكَ
وَهُوَ كَبَائِعِ سَيْفٍ لِقَاطِعِ طَرِيقٍ.²

Therefore know, You who are avid for knowledge
and who have a sincere desire and excessive thirst
for it, that if your intention in seeking knowledge is
rivalry, boasting, surpassing your peers, drawing

---

2. Al-Ghazālī, *Bidāyat al-Hidāyah*, p. 8.

people's attention to you, and amassing the vanities of this world, then you are in reality in the process of ruining your religion, destroying yourself and selling your Hereafter in exchange for this worldly life—your transaction would therefore be an utter loss, and your trading profitless. [In such a case] your teacher would also be helping you in disobeying Allah and is your partner in loss, just like the person who sells a sword to a highway robber.*

*T*his quotation is from Imām al-Ghazālī's *Bidāyat al-Hidāyah* (*The Beginning of Guidance*), a small work which captures the essence of *Iḥyāʾ ʿUlūm al-Dīn* (*The Revival of the Religious Sciences*), to which there are many cross-references.

Scholarship is laden with spiritual traps because it can nourish and sustain egotism. It can also lead to negative competition, showing off, and self-aggrandisement. Imām al-Ghazālī also warns against scholarship which is solely sought as a ticket to gain material wealth and accumulate what he described as the wreckage of this world. Every new thing that is desired in the world of commodities carries the mark of finitude. Every new thing, whether natural or artificial, has an expiry date and is destined to wither away. In the words of Rābiʿah al-ʿAdawiyyah, 'All that which is on the surface of dust is dust itself!'

---

* Muhammad Abul Quasem, *Al-Ghazali on Islamic Guidance*, 1979, p.18 (Modified).

Elsewhere, Imām al-Ghazālī says that if you were to find yourself on a sinking ship, you would only take with you things that could help keep you alive! Carrying your weighty belongings, even if they were of gold in such a situation is definitely not wise. Likewise, it is your good deeds (and bad ones too!) that continue with you after death. Your good deeds are your boat to safety!

Though Imām al-Ghazālī is here warning the students of knowledge who aim at occupying public offices, such as becoming a judge or an imam, everyone can benefit from checking their intentions, whether one studies the exact sciences, the humanities or art. There may still be room for egotism or ill intention in seeking any kind of knowledge or position, even when it apparently complies with Islamic law.

One should not be casual about what one is doing or why one is doing it. The challenge is to be God-conscious, watch one's heart carefully to detect the residues of 'I' and cleanse one's heart of such impurities. This is why one seeks refuge in Allah against associating anything or anyone with Him. Muslims are very careful about idol-worship when the idol is physical, but the same should be applied to metaphorical idols such as fame and wealth. This is why the Sufis talk about the state of annihilation (*fanā'*) whereby the heart is only aware of the Divine presence and nothing else.

Seek Felicity

السَّعَادَةُ الأُخْرَوِيَّةُ الَّتِي نَعْنِي بِهَا بَقَاءٌ بِلاَ فَنَاءٍ، وَلَذَّةٌ بِلاَ عَنَاءٍ،
وَسُرُورٌ بِلاَ حُزْنٍ، وَغِنًى بِلاَ فَقْرٍ، وَكَمَالٌ بِلاَ نُقْصَانٍ، وَعِزٌّ
بِلاَ ذُلٍّ. وَبِالجُمْلَةِ: كُلُّ مَا يُتَصَوَّرُ أَنْ يَكُونَ مَطْلُوبًا طَالِبًا،
وَمَرْغُوبًا رَاغِبًا، وَذَلِكَ أَبَدَ الآبَادِ، عَلَى وَجْهٍ لاَ تُنْقِصُهُ تَصَرُّمُ
الأَحْقَابِ وَالآجَالِ. بَلْ لَوْ قَدَّرْنَا الدُّنْيَا مَمْلُوءَةً بِالدُّرَرِ، وَقَدَّرْنَا
طَائِرًا يَخْتَطِفُ فِي كُلِّ أَلْفِ سَنَةٍ حَبَّةً وَاحِدَةً مِنْهَا، لَفَنِيَتِ
الدُّرَرُ وَلَمْ يَنْقُصْ مِنْ أَبَدِ الآبَادِ شَيْءٌ.[3]

The otherworldly felicity we are concerned with is
subsistence without end, pleasure without toil, happiness
without sadness, richness without impoverishment, perfection without blemish and glory without humiliation.
In sum, it is everything that can [at the same time] be
conceived of as sought and seeking, desired and desirous,
eternally and forever, such that it is undiminished by the
passage of time and successions of generations.

---

3. Al-Ghazālī, *Mīzān al-ʿAmal*, edited by Sulaymān Dunyā,
Cairo: Dār al-Maʿārif, 1964, pp. 180–181.

Indeed, if the whole world was full of gems and a bird was to pilfer one of them every one thousand years, then the gems would be exhausted but everlasting eternity would not be diminished a bit.*

No matter how plentiful they are, the good and enjoyable things in this world are finite. In fact, even the bad things are finite. Worldly pleasures, often conflated with happiness, are dependent on finite components. Even when they are wholesome and there is nothing controversial about them, or about how they are acquired, they are always incomplete and lacking. Material fulfilment is temporary in its very nature and the physical pleasures cannot be maintained, even when wealth and good health are at one's disposal. One cannot eat continuously, for example, because food is plentiful and tasty, even if one does not care about health issues. Eating continuously is not sustainable. Everything that one builds will inevitably wither away in time, and all those beloved to one will either leave one or one will leave them, just as all accumulated wealth, big or small, will one day be left behind. It is foolish to prefer what is finite and perishable to everlasting life,

---

* Being a translation of a chapter from Abū Ḥāmid al-Ghazālī's *Criterion of Action (Mīzān al-ʿAmal)* Ed. By S. Dunyā (Dār al-Maʿārif Press, Cairo, 1964) pp. 180-181. Translation by Muhammad Hozien, modified by Mustafa abu Sway.

perpetual happiness and infinite rewards, where no effort is required. An abode where there is no striving or toil, where all joys are eternal, without any negative associations as in this worldly life.

It is important not to confuse wealth with the state of happiness. Material wealth does not translate necessarily into happiness, for there are many people who are comfortable financially yet lead a miserable life. Many of them end up committing suicide due to a lack of meaning in their lives. Yet, material wealth does not necessarily preclude happiness, nor could it be automatically considered antithetical to a fulfilling spiritual life. It all depends on what is going on in one's heart, and not on what is available in one's bank account. The heart may be obsessed with material wealth to the extent that this prevents one from tending to one's spiritual needs.

Muslims are, for instance, enjoined to perform the Pilgrimage to Makkah and circumambulate the Kaʿbah, the first house established for the worship of Allah. This pillar of Islam is required once in a Muslim's lifetime if he or she is capable financially and physically. Yet, many choose to circumambulate the malls and the marketplaces time and again, often buying unnecessary things, or simply walking around as if time is not the most precious 'commodity'. What is life if not the sum of these moments, whether utilised properly or not? But leading a purposeless life is not about time, it is about the path one charts. Not using time properly is an act of ingratitude towards Allah who has gifted one with life. Is death not an end to time in this life? Is wasting time not a kind of death of the wasted months and years? Why, then, does one lament and feel a deep sense of sorrow for the former form of death but not lament or feel a deep sense of sorrow for the latter form?

4

Introspection

ثُمَّ لَاحَظْتُ أَحْوَالِي، فَإِذَا أَنَا مُنْغَمِسٌ فِي الْعَلَائِقِ، وَقَدْ
أَحْدَقَتْ بِي مِنَ الْجَوَانِبِ، وَلَاحَظْتُ أَعْمَالِي- وَأَحْسَنُهَا
التَّدْرِيسُ والتَّعْلِيمُ- فَإِذَا أَنَا مُقْبِلٌ عَلَى عُلُومٍ غَيْرِ مُهِمَّةٍ،
وَلَا نَافِعَةٍ فِي طَرِيقِ الْآخِرَةِ. ثُمَّ تَفَكَّرْتُ فِي نِيَّتِي فِي التَّدْرِيسِ،
فَإِذَا هِيَ غَيْرُ صَالِحَةٍ لِوَجْهِ اللهِ تَعَالَى، بَلْ بَاعِثُهَا وَمُحَرِّكُهَا طَلَبُ
الْجَاهِ وَانْتِشَارُ الصِّيتِ؛ فَتَيَقَّنْتُ أَنِّي عَلَى شَفَا جُرُفٍ هَارٍ
وَأَنِّي قَدْ أَشْفَيْتُ عَلَى النَّارِ إِنْ لَمْ أَشْتَغِلْ بِتَلَافِي الْأَحْوَالِ.⁴

Then I considered my state of affairs, and I realised that
I was deep in worldly attachments, surrounding me
as they were from every side. I then scrutinised all my
works, teaching and instructing being the finest among
these, and I found that I was occupied with unimportant
disciplines, since they were of no benefit for the way
to the Hereafter. Then I meditated on my intention in

---

4. Al-Ghazālī, *al-Munqidh min al-Ḍalāl*, edited by Jamīl Ṣalībā
and Kāmil ʿAyyād, Dār al-Andalus, 1981, p. 134.

teaching and realised that my intention was not purely
for the sake of Allah Most High. In fact, my intention
was spurred and motivated by seeking status and fame.
I became therefore certain that I was on the verge of
a deep precipice, almost plunging into hellfire unless I
worked to remedy my state of affairs.*

*I*f one word could capture Imām al-Ghazālī's solution
to the worldly attachments and distractions that
prevented him from turning wholeheartedly towards
Allah, it is *detachment*. To attain eternal felicity, he
had to reach piety and detach his heart from tending
to vain activity and, indeed, from worldliness. He
had to forgo money and fame and the source of
all this: his position at the Niẓāmiyyah College of
Baghdad. Why, then, did he return to teaching after
he 'disappeared' for eleven years?

What al-Ghazālī did is still unique even today, his
story continues to be a reminder of what it takes to
detach oneself from worldly affairs and things. He
literally gave up his teaching position (his younger
brother Aḥmad replaced him at the Niẓāmiyyah),
distributed his wealth and left Baghdad first to
Damascus and then to other cities, keeping his
identity hidden from others to get rid of fame and its

---

* *Al-Munqidh min al-Ḍalāl*, translated by Muhammad Abulaylah
[edited by George F. McLean], Council for Research in Values
and Philosophy, 2002.

adverse effects on the heart. In the language of the Sufis, he was in a state of *khumūl*, the antithesis of fame. He wanted his heart to settle down by being unknown.

He had to redirect himself towards Allah, for if he did not return to the path that leads to Him, he would be squandering his chance to reach his eternal destination. One can imagine people driving on a road, certain that that road will lead them straight to their beloved ones, only to realise after a while that they were on the wrong road, and that they would need to make a U-Turn. Had they paid attention to the road signs, they would not have lost precious time, but it is never too late. Such people do not hesitate to change course once they realise they are on the wrong course, and they might even try to make up for lost time.

There is a Sufi imam at the Dome of the Rock at Al-Aqsa Mosque in Jerusalem who keeps making a supplication asking Allah not to allow *alterities* to cut him (and the congregation) off Allah. As to what constitutes alterities, it is all creation. This is a profound supplication from someone who desires to be 'connected', which is the etymology and essence of the word *ṣalāh*, through the prayer. The heart can accommodate one thing or another, but not two things at the same time.

5

Do Your Good Deeds Outnumber Your Bad Ones?

وَإِذَا عَمِلَ طَاعَةً حَفِظَهَا وَاعْتَدَّ بِهَا كَالَّذِي يَسْتَغْفِرُ بِلِسَانِهِ أَوْ يُسَبِّحُ فِي اللَّيْلِ وَالنَّهَارِ مَثَلاً مِائَةَ مَرَّةٍ أَوْ أَلْفَ مَرَّةٍ ثُمَّ يَغْتَابُ الْمُسْلِمِينَ وَيَتَكَلَّمُ بِمَا لَا يَرْضَاهُ اللهُ طُولَ النَّهَارِ وَيَلْتَفِتُ إِلَى مَا وَرَدَ فِي فَضْلِ التَّسْبِيحِ. وَيَغْفُلُ عَمَّا وَرَدَ فِي عُقُوبَةِ الْمُغْتَابِينَ وَالْكَذَّابِينَ وَالنَّمَّامِينَ وَالْمُنَافِقِينَ. وَذَلِكَ مَحْضُ الْغُرُورِ. فَحِفْظُ لِسَانِهِ عَنِ الْمَعَاصِي آكَدُ مِنْ تَسْبِيحَاتِهِ.[5]

And if he performs an act of obedience, he remembers it and takes pride in it, yet he is like someone who seeks [Allah's] forgiveness with his tongue or glorifying [Allah] at night or during the day one hundred times or one

---

5. Al-Ghazālī, *al-Kashf wa al-Tabyīn* [*Aṣnāf al-Maghrūrīn*], ed. by ʿAbd al-Laṭīf ʿĀshūr, Cairo: Maktabat al-Qurʾān, p. 31.

thousand times, but then he backbites the Muslims and
throughout the day utters that which displeases Allah,
and [only] pays attention to the narrations on the merit
of glorification [of Allah] while neglecting the reports on
the punishment of backbiters, liars, tale-bearers
and hypocrites. This is pure self-delusion, for
protecting his tongue from disobediences is
more urgent than his glorifications.

*I*mām al-Ghazālī is fully aware of the contradiction
between healthy acts of worship and vice. An example
is a person who repeatedly seeks Allah's forgiveness,
day and night, yet does not control his tongue when
it comes to backbiting. People remember their own
good deeds and take pride in them while they have,
at the same time, no reservations or hesitation about
bad behaviour. How can they use the tongue for
both: extolling Allah's name and speaking badly
about other people?

Abstaining from sin takes precedence over doing
any good action. Repentance means having the
intention not to engage in the acts that are prohibited,
even if one happens to relapse later to bad old habits.

To be truly God-conscious means one should
recognise that whatever good one performs, it is
because of Divine guidance, and whatever and
whenever wrong deeds are avoided, it is because of
Divine protection.

There are a few problems associated with doing good or evil. The first problem with doing good is attributing it to oneself, rather than seeing oneself as an agent who has been guided to do what is good. The other problem is only seeing the good deeds and not the bad ones which may outweigh the good ones. It is a kind of whitewashing one's records, constructing an image that does not reflect the inner reality.

The problem with doing evil or mistakes is not taking responsibility for them or taking action to correct the situation. While mistakes are inevitable, repentance should always be immediate and sincere.

The Greatest
Pleasure of All

إِنَّ اللَّذَّةَ وَالسَّعَادَةَ لِابْنِ آدَمَ مَعْرِفَةُ اللهِ سُبْحَانَهُ وَتَعَالَى. اِعْلَمْ أَنَّ
سَعَادَةَ كُلِّ شَيْءٍ وَلَذَّتَهُ وَرَاحَتَهُ تَكُونُ بِمُقْتَضَى طَبْعِهِ، وَطَبْعُ كُلِّ
شَيْءٍ مَا خُلِقَ لَهُ؛ فَلَذَّةُ الْعَيْنِ فِي الصُّوَرِ الْحَسَنَةِ، وَلَذَّةُ الْأُذُنِ فِي
الْأَصْوَاتِ الطَّيِّبَةِ. وَكَذَلِكَ سَائِرُ الْجَوَارِحِ بِهَذِهِ الصِّفَةِ. وَلَذَّةُ
الْقَلْبِ خَاصَّةٌ بِمَعْرِفَةِ اللهِ سُبْحَانَهُ وَتَعَالَى لِأَنَّهُ مَخْلُوقٌ لَهَا.[6]

Verily, pleasure and felicity for the son of Adam lie in
knowing Allah, glorified and exalted is He. Know that
the felicity of everything, its pleasure and its comfort, is
according to its nature, and the nature of everything is
that which it was created for. Hence the pleasure of the
eye is in beautiful forms, and the pleasure of the ear is in
wholesome sounds, and so are the pleasures of the rest
of the limbs according to this quality. And the exclusive

---

6. Al-Ghazālī, *Kimyā' al-Saʿādah*, edited by Muhammad ʿAbd
al-ʿAlīm, Cairo: Maktabat al-Qur'ān, p. 51.

pleasure of the heart is knowing Allah, glorified and
exalted is He, for it is created for that.

*P*hilosophers and theologians differed for millennia
over the meaning of felicity, and they came up with
interesting definitions, from being the ultimate
purpose in life for Aristotle to the modern American
pursuit of happiness, where it is measured against
material tangible gains. Sometimes happiness is used
loosely to indicate that one is having fun or a good
time. This is reductionist at best!

In general, associating happiness with pleasure,
wealth and status is wrong. While one does need
real things to survive, they cannot be the criterion
of happiness. It is even worse when happiness is
constructed as organically rooted in consumerism.
This leads people to continuously buy and consume
things in order to be happy, and this has its own toll
on the human psyche. It may even become a source
of misery.

Imām al-Ghazālī, in *Iḥyā' ʿUlūm al-Dīn*, states
that human beings do not fulfil the purpose of life by
biological activities, or physical traits, for there are
animals that eat more, or are stronger or have bigger
bodies, etc. The human being is created to worship
Allah. Everything else is an accessory!

Here, Imām al-Ghazālī provides an interesting
narrative about pleasure and happiness, where each

organ finds its own 'happiness' in a life that fits its nature. The eye finds pleasure in beautiful forms and the ear in beautiful sounds. As for the heart, its source of happiness is knowing Allah. Elsewhere in the *Iḥyā'*, al-Ghazālī stated that the heart has only been created to know Allah. This knowledge necessitates an intimate knowledge of the Qur'ān, Allah's message to humanity at large.

It follows that there is no happiness without knowing Allah. It does not matter whom and what you know apart from Allah. One may know the names of football players or actors or musicians, as is the case with many people today, but ultimately this knowledge does not help in the godly pursuit of happiness. Many of these stars lead unhappy lives that are the epitome of misery: gambling, drug addiction, alcoholism and, sadly, suicide.

In the Greek and modern western worldviews, happiness is here and now. In Islam, happiness encompasses two realms, life on earth and in the Hereafter. The real happy and felicitous person is the one who makes it to Paradise.

Deconstructing Greek Metaphysics

لِيُعْلَمَ أَنَّ الْمَقْصُودَ تَنْبِيهُ مَنْ حَسُنَ اعْتِقَادُهُ فِي الْفَلَاسِفَةِ، وَظَنَّ أَنَّ
مَسَالِكَهُم نَقِيَّةٌ عَنِ التَّنَقُّضِ، بِبَيَانِ وُجُوهِ تَهَافُتِهِم، فَلِذَلِكَ لَا أَدْخُلُ
فِي الِاعْتِرَاضِ عَلَيْهِم إِلَّا دُخُولَ مُطَالِبٍ مُنْكِرٍ، لَا دُخُولَ مُدَّعٍ
مُثْبِتٍ؛ فَأُبْطِلُ عَلَيْهِم مَا اعْتَقَدُوهُ مَقْطُوعًا بِالْإِلْزَامَاتِ مُخْتَلِفَةٍ،
فَأُلْزِمُهُم تَارَةً مَذْهَبَ الْمُعْتَزِلَةِ وَأُخْرَى مَذْهَبَ الْكَرَّامِيَّةِ؛
وَطَوْرًا مَذْهَبَ الْوَاقِفِيَّةِ، وَلَا أَنْهَضُ ذَابًا عَنْ مَذْهَبٍ مَخْصُوصٍ
بَلْ أَجْعَلُ جَمِيعَ الْفِرَقِ إِلْبًا واحِدًا عَلَيْهِم، فَإِنَّ سَائِرَ الْفِرَقِ
رُبَّمَا خَالَفُونَا فِي التَّفْصِيلِ، وَهَؤُلَاءِ يَتَعَرَّضُونَ لِأُصُولِ الدِّينِ،
فَلْنَتَظَاهَرْ عَلَيْهِم فَعِنْدَ الشَّدَائِدِ تَذْهَبُ الْأَحْقَادُ. [7]

Let it be known that the purpose is to warn those
who think well of the philosophers, and consider their

---

7. Al-Ghazālī, *Tahāfut al-Falāsifah*, edited by Sulaymān Dunyā,
Cairo: Dār al-Maʿārif, 1972, pp. 82–83.

methods to be flawless, by elucidating the aspects of their incoherence. This is why my objection to their views is by way of demanding proofs and refuting their views, and not by claiming a certain position and then proceeding to prove it. Thus, I will refute what they believe to be categorical through different compelling proofs, sometimes using the compelling proofs of the Muʿtazilah, sometimes those of the Karrāmiyyah, the Wāqifiyyah, etc. In the process, I will not defend any particular group, rather I will use all of them together against the philosophers. For all these groups differ with us in matters of details; whereas the philosophers attack the principles of our religion. Let us, therefore, unite against them; for when hardships befall grudges disappear.*

*I*mām al-Ghazālī responded to the challenges of his age. These challenges came from three sources: Greek philosophy, deviant theological trends and groups that evolved within the Islamic world, and the lack of sincerity and spirituality. One can say that essentially Muslims were, throughout their history, exposed to three essential challenges: external intellectual trends, internal schisms and ignoring the affairs of the heart. The latter is not addressed in the above quotation.

Imām al-Ghazālī divided the Greek heritage into several areas. He had no problem with logic,

---

* Al-Ghazālī, *Tahāfut Al-Falāsifah*, translated by Sabih Ahmad Kamali, Pakistan Philosophical Congress, Lahore, 1963, p. 8.

mathematics or physics. He only rejected Greek metaphysics and systematically refuted it on account of twenty points in *Tahāfut al-Falāsifah*.

The three theological/philosophical trends that he mentioned in the third preface are but examples of what he attempted to deconstruct. The Muʿtazilites were Muslim rational theologians who differed in their views with traditional Islamic theology who continued to hold the Qur'ān and the Sunnah as the primary sources for the Islamic worldview, including law and theology. The Muʿtazilites believed that reason can independently reach truths such as the knowledge of what is good and evil, without reference to revelation. The Karrāmiyyah was an offshoot of the Seventh-Imāmī Ismāʿīlī Shīʿah. They believed that Allah's essence has a corporeal reality. The Wāqifiyyah, also a Seventh-Imāmī Shīʿī sect, non-existent today, believed in the absolute unknowability of Allah.

Al-Ghazālī wrote several books and treatises attacking the esotericists (i.e., the Batinites). The latter formed the strongest political challenge to law and order during his time, for they led an assassination campaign against Sunnī political officials and scholars.

What is remarkable about al-Ghazālī's critique of the philosophers is that he was doing this on behalf of all Muslims regardless of their specific school of law or theology, and he also wanted to unite them under one banner. He was already considering these sects outside the pale of Islam, because they differed substantially on major issues of theology. The three most important issues that al-Ghazālī would not tolerate were the philosophers' belief in the eternity of the world, that Allah does not know accidents, and their denial of bodily resurrection on the Day of Judgement.

8

Do not Eat Your Path to Heaven

فَإِنَّ مَقْصَدَ ذَوِي الْأَلْبَابِ لِقَاءُ اللهِ تَعَالَى فِي دَارِ الثَّوَابِ،
وَلَا طَرِيقَ إِلَى الْوُصُولِ لِلِقَاءِ اللهِ إِلَّا بِالْعِلْمِ وَالْعَمَلِ وَلَا تُمْكِنُ
الْمُوَاظَبَةُ عَلَيْهِمَا إِلَّا بِسَلَامَةِ الْبَدَنِ وَلَا تَصْفُو سَلَامَةُ الْبَدَنِ
إِلَّا بِالْأَطْعِمَةِ وَالْأَقْوَاتِ، وَالتَّنَاوُلِ مِنْهَا بِقَدْرِ الْحَاجَةِ عَلَى
تِكْرَارِ الْأَوْقَاتِ، فَمِنْ هذَا الْوَجْهِ قَالَ بَعْضُ السَّلَفِ الصَّالِحِينَ:
إِنَّ الْأَكْلَ مِنَ الدِّينِ، وَعَلَيْهِ نَبَّهَ رَبُّ الْعَالَمِينَ بِقَوْلِهِ وَهُوَ
أَصْدَقُ الْقَائِلِينَ: (كُلُوا مِنَ الطَّيِّبَاتِ وَاعْمَلُوا صَالِحًا) فَمَنْ
يُقْدِمُ عَلَى الْأَكْلِ لِيَسْتَعِينَ بِهِ عَلَى الْعِلْمِ وَالْعَمَلِ وَيَقْوَى بِهِ
عَلَى التَّقْوَى فَلَا يَنْبَغِي أَنْ يَتْرُكَ نَفْسَهُ مُهْمَلًا سُدًى، يَسْتَرْسِلُ

فِي الْأَكْلِ اسْتِرْسَالَ الْبَهَائِمِ فِي الْمَرْعَى، فَإِنَّ مَا هُوَ ذَرِيعَةٌ
إِلَى الدِّينِ وَوَسِيلَةٌ إِلَيْهِ يَنْبَغِي أَنْ تَظْهَرَ أَنْوَارُ الدِّينِ عَلَيْهِ.⁸

The aim of those who possess sound minds is meeting
Allah Most High in the Abode of Reward [i.e. the
Hereafter], and there is no way leading to Him except
through knowledge and action, and it is not possible to
maintain these except with a healthy body, and this is
not feasible except with food and provisions, partaking
of them according to one's need, with the passage of
time. It is from this perspective that one of the righteous
Predecessors said: 'Eating is part of the religion.' The
Lord of the Worlds brought this to our attention saying:
Eat you pure food, and perform good actions (Qur'ān
23:51). Therefore, he who approaches food in order
to assist himself in seeking knowledge and doing good
deeds and strengthen himself in piety should not neglect
himself, eating excessively, like grazing animals in
pastures, for that which leads to religion and is a path
to it should have the lights of religion reflected on it.

*I*mām al-Ghazālī brings forth in the above passage the
highest aim of one's life: meeting Allah, Most High.
Proper knowledge and good action are prerequisites
for such a sublime meeting. Imām al-Ghazālī made
one qualification, which is the aim of the wise. For

---

8. Al-Ghazālī, *Iḥyā' ʿUlūm al-Dīn*, edited by Sulaymān Dunyā,
Beirut: Dār al-Maʿrifah, vol. 2, p. 2.

those who are not wise may be distracted from Allah by something of His creation. They may also drop this aim altogether precisely because they think they are wise, adopting for example a reductionist, logical positivist approach, thinking that what cannot be tested in a scientific laboratory does not exist. They might not see the whole picture of a sophisticated and well-organised vast universe that cannot possibly be the product of chance. Wise indeed is he who sees the Creator through His creation, submits to His will and follows the right path of action that leads to meeting Him on the Day of Judgement.

Modern life is distracting and overwhelming, but one should transform one's life into a spiritually fulfilling one. Every act can become wholesome if it is done for the sake of Allah. This includes having food to sustain oneself, but also with the intention to utilise the energy acquired to worship Allah and to serve Him as well as to serve oneself, the community and humanity at large. This would fulfil the import of the Qur'ānic verse that advocates eating wholesome food, only to be followed by good righteous action.

Eating, therefore, has been considered a religious act because of the good associated with it. Refraining from eating enough or eating well, when it prevents one from performing one's duties, becomes prohibited. Consumption of food, Imām al-Ghazālī warns, should not lead to overeating in a manner similar to animals. For he wanted spirituality to be part of the picture. The Prophetic practice teaches us that nothing that the human being fills is worse than his stomach, and that the proper amount of food intake is a third for food, a third for drink and a third for air.

Overeating leads to all kinds of health problems. It should also be remembered that overeating takes place at the expense of those who do not have enough to eat.

9

The Merits of Marriage

اِعْلَمْ أَنَّ الْعُلَمَاءَ قَدِ اخْتَلَفُوا فِي فَضْلِ النِّكَاحِ فَبَالَغَ بَعْضُهُمْ فِيهِ
حَتَّى زَعَمَ أَنَّهُ أَفْضَلُ مِنَ التَّخَلِّي لِعِبَادَةِ اللهِ وَاعْتَرَفَ آخَرُونَ
بِفَضْلِهِ وَلَكِنِ قَدَّمُوا عَلَيْهِ التَّخَلِّي لِعِبَادَةِ اللهِ، مَهْمَا لَمْ تَتُقْ
النَّفْسُ إِلَى النِّكَاحِ تَوَقَانَاً يُشَوِّشُ الْحَالَ وَيَدْعُو إِلَى الْوِقَاعِ.

Know that the scholars have differed about the merit of
marriage, with some of them exaggerating its merit to
the extent that they claimed it is better than dedicating
oneself to the worship of Allah; while others recognised
its merit but preferred dedicating oneself to the worship of Allah over it, as long as one does not long for
marriage to such an extent that it disturbs
one's state and tempts one to have sex.

---

9. Al-Ghazālī, *Iḥyā' ʿUlūm al-Dīn*, edited by Sulaymān Dunyā,
Beirut: Dār al-Maʿrifah, p. 21.

*T*here is no doubt that marriage is meritorious, and that it is the normative Prophetic path, so much so that by getting married it is considered that one has fulfilled half of one's religion. But there has to be a correlation between marriage and spirituality. This is why Imām al-Ghazālī mentions those scholars who thought of marriage as a preferred action compared to being in a retreat dedicated to the worship of Allah. Other scholars reversed this order, whereby dedicating oneself to the worship of Allah is, for them, better than marriage as long as one's heart is not preoccupied with sexual desires.

Marriage shields one from wrongdoing when it goes hand in hand with other teachings pertaining to sexuality, such as lowering one's gaze, for both men and women, and avoiding being in seclusion with the opposite sex. The Prophet 🌸 wanted young people to get married if they could afford it, otherwise they needed to fast, for fasting eliminates lust. The Prophet 🌸 stated that marriage is part of his Sunnah. In fact, the Qur'ān does say that Allah never prescribed celibacy. (Qur'ān 57:27)

The Prophet 🌸 also encouraged Muslims to get married and procreate, for offspring is a necessary condition for the continuation of life on earth, and this is why the protection of progeny is one of the main objectives of the Sacred law (*maqāṣid al-sharīʿah*). Marriage in the Qur'ān is, in its essence, a bond of peacefulness, harmony, tranquillity and mercy: *And of His signs is that He created for you from yourselves mates that you may find tranquillity in them, and He fashioned between you affection and mercy. Indeed, in that are signs for a people who give thought.* (Qur'ān 30:21) This tranquillity is entrenched in equal rights and responsibilities. The Prophet ﷺ used to perform house chores. Therefore, such work is genderless.

In addition to physical attraction, the Prophet ﷺ emphasised religiosity in one's choice of a spouse, both for men and women. Because fornication and adultery are grave sins, the opposite is also true. Sexual relations between spouses is a good deed.

10

Striving Beyond Justice

وَقَدْ أَمَرَ اللهُ تَعَالَى بِالْعَدْلِ وَالْإِحْسَانِ جَمِيعاً، وَالْعَدْلُ سَبَبُ
النَّجَاةِ فَقَطْ، وَهُوَ يَجْرِي مِنَ التِّجَارَةِ مَجْرَى رَأْسِ الْمَالِ.
وَالْإِحْسَانُ سَبَبُ الْفَوْزِ وَنَيْلِ السَّعَادَةِ، وَهُوَ يَجْرِي مِنَ التِّجَارَةِ
مَجْرَى الرِّبْحِ، وَلَا يُعَدُّ مِنَ الْعُقَلَاءِ مَنْ قَنِعَ فِي مُعَامَلَاتِ الدُّنْيَا
بِرَأْسِ مَالِهِ، فَكَذَا فِي مُعَامَلَاتِ الْآخِرَةِ، فَلَا يَنْبَغِي لِلْمُتَدِيِّنِ أَنْ
يَقْتَصِرَ عَلَى الْعَدْلِ وَاجْتِنَابِ الظُّلْمِ وَيَدَعَ أَبْوَابَ الْإِحْسَانِ،
وَقَدْ قَالَ اللهُ: وَأَحْسِنْ كَمَا أَحْسَنَ اللهُ إِلَيْكَ وَقَالَ عَزَّ وَجَلَّ:
إِنَّ اللهَ يَأْمُرُ بِالْعَدْلِ وَالْإِحْسَانِ وَقَالَ سُبْحَانَهُ: إِنَّ رَحْمَةَ اللهِ
قَرِيبٌ مِنَ الْمُحْسِنِينَ وَنَعْنِي بِالْإِحْسَانِ فِعْلَ مَا يَنْفَعُ بِهِ الْمُعَامَلُ
وَهُوَ غَيْرُ وَاجِبٍ عَلَيْهِ، وَلَكِنَّهُ تَفَضُّلٌ مِنْهُ، فَإِنَّ الْوَاجِبَ
يَدْخُلُ فِي بَابِ الْعَدْلِ وَتَرْكِ الظُّلْمِ وَقَدْ ذَكَرْنَاهُ.[10]

---

10.   Al-Ghazālī, *Iḥyā' ʿUlūm al-Dīn*, edited by Sulaymān Dunyā,
Beirut: Dār al-Maʿrifah, vol. 2, p. 79.

Allah Most High enjoins justice and excellence. Justice is the cause of salvation only, and it is likened to capital in trade. Excellence, on the other hand, is the cause of success and felicity, and it is likened to profit in trade.

Anyone who is satisfied with only his capital when trading in worldly affairs cannot be considered a sane person. The same applies to all dealings pertaining to the Hereafter. The religious person should not confine himself to justice and avoiding injustice, while shunning the doors of excellence. Allah said: *...And do good as Allah has done good to you...* (Qur'ān 28:77), *Indeed, Allah orders justice and excellence...* (Qur'ān 16:90), and He also said: *...Indeed, the mercy of Allah is near to the doers of good* (Qur'ān 7:56). And we mean by excellence, doing that which benefits the person one is dealing with, without this being obligatory on him, but rather out of courtesy, for that which is obligatory is addressed under the rubric of justice and abandoning injustice, and this has already been mentioned.

*J*ustice in Islam is the cornerstone of every institution, including the family, the community and the state. It is a key factor in being accepted by Allah, Who commanded humanity to be just and to do charitable and beautiful good deeds (*iḥsān*). Prophets and messengers were sent to humanity, along with their revealed scriptures, so that justice prevails: *We have already sent Our messengers with clear evidences and sent down with them the Scripture and the balance that the people may maintain [their affairs] in justice...* (Qur'ān 57:25)

Justice, as Imām al-Ghazālī explains, is the capital that we have, and excellence is the profit. It is imperative to be just, to end existing injustice and to prevent it from taking place. Justice is dispensed on equal terms to Muslims and non-Muslims, to men and women, to friends and foes. One should guard against favouritism, which runs against justice. On the other hand, the Qur'ān warns Muslims against bias in case one suffers at the hands of a specific group: *O you who have believed, be persistently standing firm for Allah, witnesses in justice, and do not let the hatred of a people prevent you from being just. Be just; that is nearer to righteousness. And fear Allah; indeed, Allah is acquainted with what you do.* (Qur'ān 5:8)

But to soar high, one needs to do that which one does not have to do. There is a need here to explain *iḥsān*, which is usually rendered in English as 'excellence' but for which there is no English equivalent. In the *ḥadīth* of the archangel Gabriel, he asks the Prophet ﷺ several questions, beginning with *Islām* (the five pillars), *Īmān* (the articles of faith), and then about *Iḥsān*, before moving on to issues pertaining to the End of Times. In explaining *Iḥsān,* the Prophet ﷺ, said: 'It is to worship Allah as though you see Him, for if you do not see Him, He nevertheless sees you.' (*Ṣaḥīḥ al-Bukhārī*, no.50)

The etymology of *Iḥsān*, from the root (*ḥ-s-n*), refers to beautiful action done to a degree of excellence. All voluntary charitable work that goes beyond justice falls within *Iḥsān*.

11

Degrees of Piety

إِنَّ الْوَرَعَ لَهُ أَوَّلٌ وَهُوَ الِامْتِنَاعُ عَمَّا حَرَّمَتْهُ الْفَتْوَى وَهُوَ وَرَعُ
الْعُدُولِ وَلَهُ غَايَةٌ وَهُوَ وَرَعُ الصِّدِّيقِينَ، وَذَلِكَ هُوَ الِامْتِنَاعُ مِنْ
كُلِّ مَا لَيْسَ لِلهِ مِمَّا أُخِذَ بِشَهْوَةٍ أَوْ تُوُصِّلَ إِلَيْهِ بِمَكْرُوهٍ،
أَوِ اتَّصَلَ بِسَبَبِهِ مَكْرُوهٌ وَبَيْنَهُمَا دَرَجَاتٌ فِي الِاحْتِيَاطِ، فَكُلَّمَا
كَانَ الْعَبْدُ أَشَدَّ تَشْدِيدا عَلَى نَفْسِهِ كَانَ أَخَفَّ ظَهْراً يَوْمَ
الْقِيَامَةِ وَأَسْرَعَ جَوَازاً عَلَى الصِّرَاطِ، وَأَبْعَدَ عَنْ أَنْ تَتَرَجَّحَ كِفَّةُ
سَيِّئَاتِهِ عَلَى كِفَّةِ حَسَنَاتِهِ وَتَفَاوَتُ الْمَنَازِلِ فِي الْآخِرَةِ
بِحَسَبِ تَفَاوُتِ هَذِهِ الدَّرَجَاتِ فِي الْوَرَعِ.[11]

Verily, the beginning of piety is abstaining from what is
prohibited by fatwa, and this is the piety of the upright
ones, but its aim is the piety of the friends of Allah,
which is abstaining from all that which is not done

---

11. Al-Ghazālī, *Iḥyāʾ ʿUlūm al-Dīn*, edited by Sulaymān Dunyā,
Beirut: Dār al-Maʿrifah, p. 98.

for the sake of Allah, including that which was taken
with lust, or obtained through reprehensible means,
or resulted in what is reprehensible, and these have
various degrees of precautionary steps between them.
The stricter the servant is with himself, the lighter his
load will be on the Day of Judgment, and the faster he
will cross the Bridge-over-Hell, and the farther he will
be from having his sins outweigh his good deeds.
The ranks [of people] in the Hereafter vary
according to these degrees of piety.

*P*ersonal taste, personal opinion and custom are
not the source of normative behaviour. There is
Revelation and there is the practical example and
model of behaviour as manifested in the life of the
Prophet ﷺ. The first degree of piety is not to cross
the boundaries set by the religion, and the higher
degrees include abandoning lawful things because
they may be bordering on that which is prohibited or
because one's intention is not for the sake of Allah.
Not only one ought to seek that which is lawful, the
means leading to it should also be lawful.

Piety is treating that which is prohibited as such.
It is submitting to the Divine Will and not seeking to
alter its nature. Gambling, for example, will never
be lawful, and there are no conditions or contexts
that will change its evil nature. Bribery, usury, theft
and white-collar crimes are all sources of prohibited
income.

One should also be alarmed about trading in prohibited food. Pork was and still is prohibited explicitly in the Torah and the Qur'ān. Jesus Christ was never reported to have eaten pork or to explicitly permit it; he upheld the Mosaic Law. Lawful meat (*ḥalāl*) is not restricted to that which is slaughtered according to Islamic law. It is also about what the animal eats and whether it is raised in a humane way. The Prophet ﷺ cared about the welfare and psychology of animals.

Piety means that one is expected to make or accept only money that is wholesome, gained by lawful means and spent in a way that pleases Allah. The economic activity should be beneficial according to Islamic norms. Opening gambling casinos may create jobs, but it is still prohibited in the Islamic worldview, because it destroys families.

Imām al-Ghazālī highlights the fact that one should be conscientious about one's source of income. People should guard against earning prohibited wealth, using prohibited means, or causing harm. Negligent behaviour in this life might lead to a prolonged reckoning in the Hereafter. Allah will ask people on the Day of Judgement about their wealth; how they earned it and what they did with it.

12

The Fruit of Divine Love

وَالمَقْصُودُ أَنَّ حُبَّ اللهِ إِذَا قَوِيَ أَثْمَرَ حُبَّ كُلِّ مَنْ يَقُومُ بِحَقِّ
عِبَادَةِ اللهِ فِي عِلْمٍ أَوْ عَمَلٍ وَأَثْمَرَ حُبَّ كُلِّ مَنْ فِيهِ صِفَةٌ مَرْضِيَّةٌ
عِنْدَ اللهِ مِنْ خُلُقٍ حَسَنٍ أَوْ تَأَدُّبٍ بِآدَابِ الشَّرْعِ. وَمَا مِنْ
مُحِبٍّ لِلآخِرَةِ وَمُحِبٍّ للهِ إِلَّا إِذَا أُخْبِرَ عَنْ حَالِ رَجُلَيْنِ
أَحَدُهُمَا عَالِمٌ عَابِدٌ وَالآخَرُ جَاهِلٌ فَاسِقٌ إِلَّا وَجَدَ فِي نَفْسِهِ
مَيْلاً إِلَى العَالِمِ العَابِدِ، ثُمَّ يَضْعُفُ ذَلِكَ المَيْلُ وَيَقْوَى بِحَسَبِ
صِنْفِ إِيمَانِهِ وَقُوَّتِهِ وَبِحَسَبِ ضُعْفِ حُبِّهِ للهِ وَقُوَّتِهِ وَهَذَا
المَيْلُ حَاصِلٌ وَإِنْ كَانَا غَانِبَيْنِ عَنْهُ بِحَيْثُ يَعْلَمُ أَنَّهُ لَا يُصِيبُهُ
مِنْهُمَا خَيْرٌ وَلَا شَرٌّ فِي الدُّنْيَا وَلَا فِي الآخِرَةِ، فَذَلِكَ المَيْلُ هُوَ
حُبٌّ فِي اللهِ وَللهِ مِنْ غَيْرِ حَظٍّ فَإِنَّهُ إِنَّمَا يُحِبُّهُ لِأَنَّ اللهَ يُحِبُّهُ

وَلِأَنَّهُ مَرْضِيٌّ عِنْدَ اللهِ تَعَالَى وَلِأَنَّهُ يُحِبُّ اللهَ تَعَالَى وَلِأَنَّهُ
مَشْغُولٌ بِعِبَادَةِ اللهِ تَعَالَى.[12]

When the love of Allah becomes strong, its fruit is the love of anyone who truly fulfils the worship of Allah in the guise of seeking knowledge or in action. Another fruit is the love of anyone who has an attribute with which Allah is pleased, including having good morals and manners acquired from the Holy Qur'ān and the Prophetic example. There is no lover of the Hereafter who loves Allah except that he when he is told about the state of two men, one knowledgeable and devout and the other ignorant and a wrongdoer, except that he will find himself inclined toward the devout and knowledgeable one. This inclination is weakened or strengthened according to the category and strength of his faith, and according to the weakness of his love of Allah or its strength. This inclination happens even when both men are absent and he knows that none of them can harm or benefit him in this world or in the Hereafter. This inclination is love in Allah and for the sake of Allah, with no personal ulterior motive involved in it at all. He loves him only because Allah loves him and is pleased with him, and because he loves Allah and is busy worshipping Allah Most High.

Imām al-Ghazālī graciously builds his argument about the love of Allah, moving from the love of the

---

12. Al-Ghazālī, *Iḥyā' ʿUlūm al-Dīn*, edited by Sulaymān Dunyā, Beirut: Dār al-Maʿrifah, p. 165.

imperfect to the love of the perfect, from the relative to the absolute, and from the material to the Divine. Once one attains Divine love, love is then extended to those who love Allah, and whom Allah loves, for they are shaped by the Prophetic example. This love is for the sake of Allah, with no expectations for personal gain. The fruit of Divine love is love. Spreading love of the good in this world is a true Islamic imperative. It is an invitation to the Prophetic fountain of love.

Love of Allah in the Qur'ān has been associated with following the Prophet ﷺ: *Say, [O Muhammad], 'If you should love Allah, then follow me, [so] Allah will love you and forgive you your sins. And Allah is Forgiving and Merciful.'* (Qur'ān 3:21)

Claims of love are verified against action. All believers within the originally monotheistic traditions, when asked whether they love Allah, will answer in the affirmative, regardless of their actions. Allah sent the prophets and messengers to be followed. They delineated the path that leads to the love of Allah. This path is intrinsically premised upon submission to the Divine Will which was revealed. Many people do the opposite in contemporary social contexts. They claim to love Allah, and yet they enact laws that legalise prohibited actions, and to a lesser extent, prohibit that which is lawful.

Those who commit mistakes and sins because of human weaknesses should not shy away from expressing their love of Allah, for He is the Forgiver.

In one of the most authentic traditions that made his Companions very happy, the Prophet 🕮 said: 'A person [in the Hereafter] is with whom he loves.' The Companions wanted to be eternally in the company of the Prophet 🕮 as well as in the company of other prophets and good people. On the human level, birds of a feather flock together all the way to the Hereafter. But there might be another meaning: If you truly love Allah, then you will be with Him.

Travelling

وَالفَوَائِدُ البَاعِثَةُ عَلَى السَّفَرِ لَا تَخْلُو مِنْ هَرَبٍ أَوْ طَلَبٍ. فَإِنَّ

المُسَافِرَ إِمَّا أَنْ يَكُونَ لَهُ مُزْعِجٌ عَنْ مَقَامِهِ وَلَوْلَاهُ لَمَا كَانَ لَهُ

مَقْصِدٌ يُسَافِرُ إِلَيْهِ، وَإِمَّا أَنْ يَكُونَ لَهُ مَقْصِدٌ وَمَطْلَبٌ. وَالهُرُوبُ

عَنْهُ إِمَّا أَمْرُهُ نِكَايَةٌ فِي الأُمُورِ الدِّينَوِيَّةِ. كَالطَّاعُونِ وَالوَبَاءِ إِذَا

ظَهَرَ بِبَلَدٍ أَوْ خَوْفٍ سَبَبُهُ فِتْنَةٌ أَوْ خُصُومَةٌ أَوْ غَلَاءُ سِعْرٍ. وَهُوَ

إِمَّا عَامٌّ كَمَا ذَكَرْنَاهُ أَوْ خَاصٌّ كَمَنْ يُقْصَدُ بِأَذِيَّةٍ فِي بَلْدَةٍ فَيَهْرُبُ

مِنْهَا. وَإِمَّا أَمْرُهُ نِكَايَةٌ فِي الدِّينِ كَمَنْ أُبْتُلِيَ فِي بَلَدِهِ بِجَاهٍ وَمَالٍ

وَاتِّسَاعِ أَسْبَابٍ تَصُدُّهُ عَنِ التَّجَرُّدِ للهِ، فَيُؤْثِرُ الغُرْبَةَ وَالخُمُولَ

وَيَجْتَنِبُ السَّعَةَ وَالجَاهَ، أَوْ كَمَنْ يُدْعَى إِلَى بِدْعَةٍ قَهْرًا أَوْ إِلَى

وِلَايَةِ عَمَلٍ لَا تَحِلُّ مُبَاشَرَتُهُ فَيَطْلُبُ الفِرَارَ مِنْهُ.[13]

The benefits that motivate travelling are either running
away from something or seeking out something, for the

---

13. Al-Ghazālī, *Iḥyāʾ ʿUlūm al-Dīn*, edited by Sulaymān Dunyā,
Beirut: Dār al-Maʿrifah, p. 245.

traveller is either bothered about something where he is staying, without which he would not aim to travel, or he has an objective and purpose in doing so. Running away takes place because of worldly issues that have adverse effects on him, such as the plague and epidemics when they appear in a country, or out of fear because of sedition, a dispute or a hike in prices. The reasons for travelling are either general, as mentioned, or particular such as being targeted with personal harm in a town so that one runs away. The reason for travelling may also be for matters detrimental to one's religion such as being tried with prominence, money and a host of other material causes that prevent one from dedicating one's time for the sake of Allah, thus preferring the life of an unknown person or a stranger to avoid wealth and status. And it may be that one is coerced to subscribe to a blameworthy innovation in religion or invited to take a public office which is unlawful to assume, and hence one flees from it.

*A*l-Ghazālī captures [in the above passage] the essence of travel. One travels to avoid danger or discomfort, to look for better conditions for one's final destination, or simply to seek some other good. There is nothing more moving than the image of refugees coming from different religious, ethnic and national backgrounds, trying to cross the Mediterranean in overcrowded boats. They ran away from war and poverty. Their plight does not end simply by reaching their new destination. If they survive the waves of the sea, the tide of xenophobia is awaiting them.

The Prophet ﷺ sent two waves of early Muslims to Abyssinia to seek refuge because Muslims were persecuted in Makkah. The Makkan idol worshippers were the first known Islamophobes. They tried unsuccessfully to poison the air between these Muslim refugees and the Negus of Ethiopia, their host.

Travelling, al-Ghazālī adds, is sought either for worldly gains or for religious purposes. The latter can be divided into seeking knowledge or action. Knowledge covers personal practical ethics that can be acquired through travelling, but also the knowledge of geography which reflects the marvels of the earth. As for action, it can be divided into acts of worship such as the formal Pilgrimage or the visitation of Makkah, Madīnah and Jerusalem.

Today, People flock to Makkah and Madīnah without hesitation, but not to Jerusalem because it is still under occupation. There is a strong scholarly argument encouraging Muslims to visit al-Aqsa Mosque because it is spiritually meritorious to do so. Imām al-Shāfiʿī, founder of the legal school to which al-Ghazālī belonged, said in one of his poems, extolling the merits of travelling:

Travel, you will find recompense for what you leave behind
And strive, for the pleasure of life is in working hard.

I have seen water stagnating when left still,
Refreshing when flowing, if not it doesn't
taste well.

Travelling may take place to avoid tribulations
and unwanted personal roles that defy Allah's
plan for humanity. Al-Ghazālī travelled to seek
knowledge, but once he became the most famous
scholar in the Muslim world, he left Baghdad in
order to purify his heart from egotistic residues
resulting from fame, money and power.

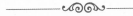

14

Listening to Songs

السَّمَاعُ قَدْ يَكُونُ حَرَاماً مَحْضاً، وَقَدْ يَكُونُ مُبَاحاً، وَقَدْ يَكُونُ
مَكْرُوهاً، وَقَدْ يَكُونُ مُسْتَحَبًّا. أَمَّا الحَرَامُ: فَهُوَ لِأَكْثَرِ النَّاسِ
مِنَ الشُّبَّانِ وَمَنْ غَلَبَتْ عَلَيْهِمْ شَهْوَةُ الدُّنْيَا فَلَا يُحَرِّكُ السَّمَاعَ
مِنْهُمْ إِلَّا مَا هُوَ الغَالِبُ عَلَى قُلُوبِهِمْ مِنَ الصِّفَاتِ المَذْمُومَةِ.
وَأَمَّا المَكْرُوهُ: فَهُوَ لِمَنْ لَا يُنَزِّلُهُ عَلَى صُورَةِ المَخْلُوقِينَ وَلَكِنَّهُ
يَتَّخِذُهُ عَادَةً لَهُ فِي أَكْثَرِ الأَوْقَاتِ عَلَى سَبِيلِ اللَّهْوِ. وَأَمَّا المُبَاحُ:
فَهُوَ لِمَنْ لَا حَظَّ لَهُ مِنْهُ إِلَّا التَّلَذُّذُ بِالصَّوْتِ الحَسَنِ.
وَأَمَّا المُسْتَحَبُّ: فَهُوَ لِمَنْ غَلَبَ عَلَيْهِ حُبُّ اللهِ تَعَالَى وَلَمْ
يُحَرِّكِ السَّمَاعَ مِنْهُ إِلَّا الصِّفَاتِ المَحْمُودَةِ.[14]

Listening [to songs] can be absolutely prohibited,
permitted, reprehensible or praiseworthy. As for
that which is prohibited, it is for most young men

---

14. Al-Ghazālī, *Iḥyā' 'Ulūm al-Dīn*, edited by Sulaymān Dunyā,
Beirut: Dār al-Maʿrifah, p. 306.

who are overwhelmed with the lust of this world; for listening will stir up in them nothing but the reviled attributes prevalent in their hearts. As for that which is reprehensible, it is for those who do not project what they listen to into the image of human beings, but take listening as a habit for most of the time, for entertainment. As for that which is permitted, it is for those whose share of listening is restricted to enjoying beautiful voices. As for that which is praiseworthy, it is for the one who is captivated by the love of Allah Most High, and listening will only stir in him his praiseworthy attributes.

*C*enturies ago one had to go to special places and gatherings to listen to songs, which were not available all the time. When Muslim scholars discussed and ruled over listening to music and songs, they could not imagine a time in the future when literally millions of recorded songs would be stored in a virtual reality that are readily available all the time. But what are they listening to?

Imām al-Ghazālī's first concern was about the content which might lead youngsters to psychological projection and fantasising about sexuality. They colour what they hear through their own lustful desires. Once the content in itself is problematic, it becomes prohibited. The degree of prohibition of this type of songs may have been more severe had the scholars of old known about some of the explicit lewd content of many songs today. And while there are songs today that may be considered positive, because they motivate people to overcome challenges and do something good, there are dark-themed songs that entertain suicide and encourage wrong behaviour.

Once the song is devoid of problematic content according to Islamic universal norms, and the listener does not project any ill thoughts, but only listens by way of habit for extended periods, then listening is reprehensible. Al-Ghazālī is concerned here with wasting time, as with any type of extended activity that does not generate personal or public good, material or spiritual. Listening here is a distraction from a purposeful life. It is interesting that the synonyms of 'entertainment' include diversion and distraction.

The third category is when listening to songs is simply permitted. Here the listener enjoys the beautiful voice and the melody. There is no transgression in content and it is done only occasionally. The fourth category is when listening becomes commendable. It is for those whom the love of Allah occupies their whole time, emotions and actions. They are the opposite of the first category, for once they hear a song about the beloved, they think of Allah. The song, in their case, becomes a tool that helps in bringing forth the best in their souls and character.

15

Enjoining Good and Forbidding Evil

فَإِنَّ الأَمْرَ بِالمَعْرُوفِ وَالنَّهْيَ عَنِ المُنْكَرِ هُوَ القُطْبُ الأَعْظَمُ
فِي الدِّينِ، وَهُوَ المُهِمُّ الذِي ابْتَعَثَ اللهُ لَهُ النَّبِيِّينَ أَجْمَعِينَ، وَلَوْ
طُوِيَ بِسَاطُهُ وَأُهْمِلَ عِلْمُهُ وَعَمَلُهُ لَتَعَطَّلَتِ النُّبُوَّةُ وَاضْمَحَلَّتِ
الدِّيَانَةُ وَعَمَّتِ الفَتْرَةُ وَفَشَتِ الضَّلَالَةُ وَشَاعَتِ الجَهَالَةُ
وَاسْتَشْرَى الفَسَادُ وَاتَّسَعَ الخَرْقُ وَخَرِبَتِ البِلَادُ، وَهَلَكَ
العِبَادُ، وَلَمْ يَشْعُرُوا بِالهَلَاكِ إِلَّا يَوْمَ التَّنَادِ. وَقَدْ كَانَ الذِي
خِفْنَا أَنْ يَكُونَ، فَإِنَّا للهِ وَإِنَّا إِلَيْهِ رَاجِعُونَ، إِذْ قَدِ انْدَرَسَ مِنْ
هذا القُطْبِ عَمَلُهُ وَعِلْمُهُ، وَانْمَحَقَ بِالكُلِّيَّةِ حَقِيقَتُهُ وَرَسْمُهُ،
فَاسْتَوْلَتْ عَلَى القُلُوبِ مُدَاهَنَةُ الخَلْقِ وَانْمَحَتْ عَنْهَا مُرَاقَبَةُ
الخَالِقِ وَاسْتَرْسَلَ النَّاسُ فِي اتِّبَاعِ الهَوَى وَالشَّهَوَاتِ اسْتِرْسَالَ
البَهَائِمِ، وَعَزَّ عَلَى بِسَاطِ الأَرْضِ مُؤْمِنٌ صَادِقٌ لَا تَأْخُذُهُ فِي اللهِ

لَوْمَةُ لَائِمٍ، فَمَنْ سَعَىٰ فِي تَلَافِي هَذِهِ الفَتْرَةِ وَسَدَّ هَذِهِ الثَّلْمَةِ إِمَّا
مُتَكَفِّلاً بِعَمَلِهَا أَوْ مُتَقَلِّداً لِتَنْفِيذِهَا مُجَدِّداً لِهَذِهِ السُّنَّةِ الدَّاثِرَةِ
نَاهِضاً بِأَعْبَائِهَا وَمُنْشَمِراً فِي إِحْيَائِهَا كَانَ مُسْتَأْثِراً مِنْ بَيْنِ
الخَلْقِ بِإِحْيَاءِ سُنَّةٍ أَفْضَى الزَّمَانُ إِلَىٰ إِمَاتَتِهَا، وَمُسْتَبِداً بِقُرْبَةٍ
تَتَضَاءَلُ دَرَجَاتُ القُرْبِ دُونَ ذِرْوَتِهَا.¹⁵

Enjoining good and forbidding evil is the greatest pillar
of religion, and it is the mission for which Allah sent all
the prophets. Had its enactment been suspended and
its knowledge and action disregarded, prophethood
would have become dysfunctional, religion would have
disappeared, slackness prevailed, misguidance spread,
ignorance common, corruption widespread, damage
irreversible, the land destroyed, and the people perished,
but they would not have realised their destruction except
on the Day of Judgment. That which we feared did
indeed take place; to Allah we belong and to Him we
shall return. The reason for this is that the knowledge
and application of this pillar has withered away, and its
reality and form erased. The hearts, therefore, have been
overcome by hypocrisy to people, while no longer being
watchful of the Creator. The people have indulged in
their whims and lusts like animals. It is rare to find on
the surface of this earth a true believer who is fearless
for the sake of Allah. Whoever takes initiative to avoid
such slackness and bridges the gap by pledging to performing it or taking the responsibility to implement it,
thus renewing this extinct Prophetic Sunnah, carrying

---

15. Al-Ghazālī, *Ihyā' ʿUlūm al-Dīn*, edited by Sulaymān Dunyā,
Beirut: Dār al-Maʿrifah, p.306.

its burdens, rolling up his sleeves to revive it—then he alone among created beings has revived a *sunnah* that time conspired to kill, and only he has exclusively obtained an act of devotion before which all other devotional acts fall short of reaching its summit.

*I*slam has essential articles of faith, pillars of worship and countless teachings on ethical and moral behaviour. Such knowledge is passed from one generation to another through formal and informal education. But once an individual or a group strays from the right path as expressed in the Islamic worldview, there is a need for a reminder. The duty to perform this reminder is described in the Qur'ān as the act of enjoining good and forbidding evil, and it is the duty of both women and men to perform it. It is the single most important criterion, along with striving on the path of Allah, which defines the Muslim *Ummah*, as described in the Qur'ān.

Though enjoining good and forbidding evil is the role of every person, there are scholars who shy away from facing people who violate clear laws and subscribe to new social trends. This is not the Prophetic path, for the prophets had the moral courage to challenge their respective communities and call them to adhere to the revealed message of Allah. This is also why no prophet was accepted with open arms. People do not like to be told what to do. More accurately, they do not want to give up bad habits and short term pleasures that contravene religion. So, for those who would like to follow the Prophetic path of enjoining good and forbidding evil, they need courage and wisdom.

The real worry of any person who censors herself or himself, and produces an appeasing narrative to address wrongdoers, or simply stops short of advocating good and forbidding evil, is to be considered a hypocrite. More than nine hundred years ago, Imām al-Ghazālī was worried about the impact of the lack of enjoining good and forbidding evil on religion. Not performing this great act will certainly diminish the religion of Islam. It will allow wrongdoers to indulge in vice so much so that they forget about Allah. Al-Ghazālī thought that the act of enjoining good and forbidding evil is a *sunnah* that has died away and he issued a call for its revival.

16

Behaviour Is the Mirror of the Heart

⟨⟨⟨⟨

فَإِنَّ آدَابَ الظَّوَاهِرِ عُنْوَانُ آدَابِ البَوَاطِنِ، وَحَرَكَاتُ الجَوَارِحِ
ثَمَرَاتُ الخَوَاطِرِ، وَالأَعْمَالُ نَتِيجَةِ الأَخْلاقِ وَالآدَابُ رَشْحُ
المَعَارِفِ، وَسَرَائِرُ القُلُوبِ هِيَ مَغَارِسُ الأَفْعَالِ وَمَنَابِعُهَا،
وَأَنْوَارُ السَّرَائِرِ هِيَ الَّتِي تُشْرِقُ عَلَى الظَّوَاهِرِ فَتُزَيِّنُهَا وَتُجَلِّيهَا،
وَتُبَدِّلُ المَحَاسِنَ مَكَارِهَهَا وَمَسَاوِيهَا. وَمَنْ لَمْ يَخْشَعْ قَلْبُهُ لَمْ
تَخْشَعْ جَوَارِحُهُ. وَمَنْ لَمْ يَكُنْ صَدْرُهُ مِشْكَاةَ الأَنْوَارِ الإِلَهِيَّةِ
لَمْ يَفِضْ عَلَى ظَاهِرِهِ جَمَالُ الآدَابِ النَّبَوِيَّةِ.[16]

Indeed, outward good manners are signs of inward
morals, and the movement of the limbs are the fruit of
inward thoughts, and deeds are the results of moral
behaviour, just as good manners are the outward sign

---

16. Al-Ghazālī, *Iḥyā' ʿUlūm al-Dīn*, edited by Sulaymān Dunyā,
Beirut: Dār al-Maʿrifah, p. 357.

of knowledge, and actions are wellsprings from the
secrets of the hearts where they are cultivated, and the
lights emanating inner sights are the ones that shine
on the outward semblance of people, making them
beautiful and polished, where the pleasant character
traits replace the reprehensible and bad ones. The person
whose heart and limbs do not submit [to Allah's will],
and whose breast is not a niche of Divine lights, the
beauty of Prophetic manners will not show on him.

External behaviour is a mirror of what is in the
heart. Manifest behaviour is the fruit of a tree that
has its roots in the heart. The heart is the field in
which one sows the seeds of all behaviour that will
become apparent in due time. One cannot display
a behaviour which is the opposite of what is in
the heart, without ultimately being exposed. If the
heart is full with the remembrance of Allah, the love
of His Prophet, and the love of neighbours, then
the outcome is peaceful activity in the service of
humanity at large. The beautiful can only produce
that which is beautiful.

We have been created to know Allah, to worship
Him and to serve humanity by adhering to the
revealed message. Reality should be appreciated when
it is right, but it should not be allowed to change our
hearts when it goes wrong. It is imperative to reject
wrongdoing and injustice committed against anyone,
Muslim or not.

The ultimate example of good external behaviour has been established in the life of the Prophet ﷺ. In order for this beautiful example to manifest itself in one's behaviour, the heart has to be the seat of Divine light. This is achievable by continuously cleansing it from worldly attachments. The heart should submit itself in its totality to the will of Allah. Daily maintenance is required because distractions and temptations are everywhere, and some influences may seep into the most conscientious hearts.

What goes on in the heart is much more important than outward behaviour, for the intentions are criteria for acceptance or rejection. When the heart is a spring of Divine love, and the limbs bathe in this spring, their outward behaviour glows in the universe.

The heart of the Muslim is at home with the message of his or her Creator. It is internally reconciled, but it also witnesses the external struggle between the various forces that exist in this universe, some of which are good and some not. This reconciled heart will always be on the side of the good, even when it looks back on history.

17

Flames of Repentance

حَدُّ التَّوبَةِ: إِنَّهَا ذَوَبَانُ الحَشَا لِمَا سَبَقَ مِنَ الخَطَأِ أَوْ نَارٌ فِي
القَلْبِ تَلْتَهِبُ، وَصَدْعٌ فِي الكَبِدِ لا يَنْشَعِبُ، وَبِاعْتِبَارِ مَعْنَى
التَّرْكِ قِيلَ فِي حَدِّ التَّوبَةِ إِنَّهُ خَلْعُ لِبَاسِ الجَفَاءِ وَنَشْرُ بِسَاطِ
الوَفَاءِ. وَقَالَ سَهْلُ بنُ عبدِ اللهِ التُّسْتَرَى: التَّوبَةُ تَبْدِيلُ
الحَرَكَاتِ المَذْمُومَةِ بِالحَرَكَاتِ المَحْمُودَةِ.[17]

Repentance is defined as the inward's aching over past
sins. It is a fire that rages in the heart and is an aching
in one's heart that cannot be shaken off. And when
taking into consideration the meaning of abstention, the
definition of repentance then becomes: it is removing the
attire of rejection and spreading the rug of loyalty. Sahl
ibn ʿAbdullāh al-Tustarī said: 'Repentance is replacing
blameworthy actions with praiseworthy actions.'

---

17. Al-Ghazālī, *Iḥyāʾ ʿUlūm al-Dīn*, edited by Sulaymān Dunyā,
Beirut: Dār al-Maʿrifah, pp. 4–5.

*T*he Prophet ﷺ said: 'All the children of Adam are sinners, and the best of sinners are those who repent.' People sin because of their human weakness, not because they are predestined to sin or it is in their nature to do so. There is also no concept of original sin in Islam, resulting from Adam and Eve eating from the Forbidden Tree in the Garden. In fact, the very first story in the Holy Qur'ān exonerates Eve from the burden of being the first one to eat from this tree. The Holy Qur'ān uses dual suffixed pronouns to refer to both Adam and Eve. So, they were both tempted and succumbed to temptation (and in a different chapter they both ate), and Satan caused their expulsion from the Garden. Adam received revealed *words* and Allah forgave him; these words explained to Adam the possibility of repentance and how to repent.

Every human being is born clean of any ancestral baggage, and everyone is responsible for his or her sins. And while it is most likely that people will sin – and that it is important to learn about sins in order to avoid them – one should know that repentance is the way out of a sinful life, and that Allah is the Forgiver, and He is also Oft-Forgiving because we sin often.

The Prophet ﷺ reprimanded one of his Companions for cursing another Companion because he drank wine, saying that 'he loves Allah and His Messenger.' This is not to encourage wrongdoing; it is to show mercy towards people who have made mistakes in their lives.

The first step of repentance is to stop doing whatever sin one is engaged in, and to have a sincere intention not to do it again, and ask Allah for forgiveness. What more encouragement does one need than this verse of the Qur'ān that promises the sinner to turn his or her sins into good deeds? *Except for those who repent, believe and do righteous work. For them Allah will replace their evil deeds with good. And ever is Allah Forgiving and Merciful.* (Qur'ān 25:70)

18

Patience in Avoiding Sin

وَأَشَدُّ أَنْوَاعِ الصَّبْرِ الصَّبْرُ عَنِ الْمَعَاصِي الَّتِي صَارَتْ مَأْلُوفَةً
بِالْعَادَةِ فَإِنَّ الْعَادَةَ طَبِيعَةٌ خَامِسَةٌ، فَإِذَا انْضَافَتِ الْعَادَةُ إِلَى
الشَّهْوَةِ تَظَاهَرَ جُنْدَانِ مِنْ جُنُودِ الشَّيْطَانِ عَلَى جُنْدِ اللهِ تَعَالَى
فَلَا يَقْوَى بَاعِثُ الدِّينِ عَلَى قَمْعِهَا، ثُمَّ إِنْ كَانَ ذَلِكَ الْفِعْلُ
مِمَّا تَيَسَّرَ فِعْلُهُ كَانَ الصَّبْرُ عَنْهُ أَثْقَلَ عَلَى النَّفْسِ، كَالصَّبْرِ عَنْ
مَعَاصِي اللِّسَانِ مِنَ الْغِيبَةِ وَالْكَذِبِ وَالْمُرَاءَاةِ وَالثَّنَاءِ عَلَى
النَّفْسِ تَعْرِيضاً وَتَصْرِيحاً. وَأَنْوَاعُ الْمَزْحِ الْمُؤْذِي لِلْقُلُوبِ
وَضُرُوبِ الْكَلِمَاتِ الَّتِي يُقْصَدُ بِهَا الِازْدِرَاءُ وَالِاسْتِحْقَارُ وَذِكْرُ
الْمَوْتَى وَالْقَدْحِ فِيهِمْ وَفِي عُلُومِهِمْ وَسِيَرِهِمْ وَمَنَاصِبِهِمْ، فَإِنَّ
ذَلِكَ فِي ظَاهِرِهِ غِيبَةٌ وَفِي بَاطِنِهِ ثَنَاءٌ عَلَى النَّفْسِ. فَلِلنَّفْسِ فِيهِ

شَهْوَتَانِ: إِحْدَاهُمَا نَفْيُ الغَيْرِ وَالأُخْرَى إِثْبَاتُ نَفْسِهِ. وَبِهَا تَتِمُّ لَهُ
الرُّبُوبِيَّةُ الَّتِي هِيَ فِي طَبْعِهِ، وَهِيَ ضِدُّ مَا أُمِرَ بِهِ مِنَ العُبُودِيَّةِ.[18]

The most difficult kind of patience is patience in avoiding
sins that have become habitually familiar, for habits
constitute a fifth nature. If habit is combined with lust,
then two soldiers of Satan have joined their forces against
the soldiers of Allah Most High, and the religious drive
would not be able to suppress them. Furthermore, if
an act of disobedience can be performed easily, then
having patience against it is more burdensome on the
self. An example is patiencethe sins of the tongue such
as backbiting, lying, showing off and praising oneself,
directly or indirectly, and also various types of joking
that hurt other people's feelings as well as any kind of
words intended for ridiculing, belittling or mentioning
the deceased while mocking their knowledge, their
conducts and their positions, for doing so is outwardly
backbiting while it is self-praise inwardly. The ego here
has two desires: one is the denial of the other, and the
other is confirming itself. Thus [by denial of others and
affirmation of the ego] one's [claim to] lordship [in
place of Allah] is made complete.Since longing for it is
in his innate nature, but it is opposite to the attitude of
servanthood one is commanded to show.

Allah praised in the Qur'ān in numerous verses those
who are patient, among which, for example, are

18. Al-Ghazālī, *Iḥyā' ʿUlūm al-Dīn*, edited by Sulaymān Dunyā,
Beirut: Dār al-Maʿrifah, p. 71.

those verses asking the Muslim community to resort to patience and the prayer for help and that, *He is with those who are patient* (Qur'ān 2:153), *to have patience and forgive [those who do ill things to them]* (Qur'ān 42:43), *to be patient like the messengers who did strive hard* (Qur'ān 46:35), *to enjoin patience* (Qur'ān 103:3), *to be patient, a goodly patience* (Qur'ān 70:5), *and that paradise is the reward for those who have patience* (Qur'ān 76:12).

Patience is the best reaction to external harm done by others. It is a virtue that requires not acting on negativity. It is the right reaction towards one's difficult socio-economic circumstances. It is the appropriate reaction towards physical pain. Imām al-Ghazālī takes patience one step further; having patience against one's desire to do wrong, especially where sinning habits have been formed. Sin and habit are two soldiers of Satan. When they go hand in hand, they have an alliance against the soldiers of Allah. They are a force to reckon with, and mere religiosity cannot uproot them. And if the sin is easy to perform, then it becomes difficult for one's self to have patience against it. Examples of sins that are difficult to prevent and easy to do include the ills of the tongue: backbiting and lying, hurtful jokes and disdain for the living and the ill mention of the dead and self-praise. All these are done by using words.

The dynamics of a healthy relationship with one-self and others is based on controlling the tongue, the abuse of which is the reason why many relations go sour. It is also the reason why many achievements are undermined because of what one says. When Muʿādh ibn Jabal asked the Prophet ﷺ about a deed that could pave his way to Paradise, the Prophet ﷺ enumerated most of the pillars of Islam, emphasising charity and performing the prayer deep into the night, yet he said that on top of everything comes restraining one's tongue is very high. The price of failing to control one's tongue loose is very high. It is tantamount to giving up one's potential place in Paradise.

19

True Grace

اِعْلَمْ أَنَّ كُلَّ خَيْرٍ وَلَذَّةٍ وَسَعَادَةٍ بَلْ كُلَّ مَطْلُوبٍ وَمُؤْثَرٍ فَإِنَّهُ
يُسَمَّى نِعْمَةً، وَلَكِنِ النِّعْمَةُ بِالْحَقِيقَةِ هِيَ السَّعَادَةُ الأُخْرَوِيَّةُ،
وَتَسْمِيَةُ مَا سِوَاهَا نِعْمَةً وَسَعَادَةً إِمَّا غَلَطٌ وَإِمَّا مَجَازٌ كَتَسْمِيَةِ
السَّعَادَةِ الدُّنْيَوِيَّةِ الَّتِي لَا تُعِينُ عَلَى الآخِرَةِ نِعْمَةً فَإِنَّ ذَلِكَ غَلَطٌ
مَحْضٌ، وَقَدْ يَكُونُ اِسْمُ النِّعْمَةِ لِلشَّيْءِ صِدْقاً وَلَكِنْ يَكُونُ
إِطْلاقُهُ عَلَى السَّعَادَةِ الأُخْرَوِيَّةِ أَصْدَقَ فَكُلُّ سَبَبٍ يُوصِلُ إِلَى
سَعَادَةِ الآخِرَةِ وَيُعِينُ عَلَيْهَا إِمَّا بِوَاسِطَةٍ وَاحِدَةٍ أَوْ بِوَسَائِطَ
فَإِنَّ تَسْمِيَتَهُ نِعْمَةً صَحِيحَةٌ وَصِدْقٌ لِأَجْلِ أَنَّهُ يُفْضِي إِلَى
النِّعْمَةِ الْحَقِيقِيَّةِ.[19]

Know that every good, every pleasure and every happiness, indeed every besought and every preferred thing, is
called a grace. Yet, true grace is happiness in the Hereafter, for calling other things 'grace' and 'happiness'

---

19. Al-Ghazālī, *Iḥyā' ʿUlūm al-Dīn*, edited by Sulaymān Dunyā,
Beirut: Dār al-Maʿrifah, p. 99.

is either a mistake or a metaphor. This is like calling worldly happiness, which does not help in the Hereafter, a grace, for this is a pure mistake. It may well be that the appellation 'grace' when applied to something is true, but this appellation applies more accurately to happiness in the Hereafter. Therefore, every cause that leads to happiness in the Hereafter, and helps to attaining it through one or more intermediaries, deserves truly and correctly to be called 'grace', for it leads to true grace.

*G*ood things can be called grace. True grace is eternal happiness. Calling things grace is either a mistake or a metaphor.

Since real happiness is only possible in the Hereafter, there is a need to evaluate and explain what we call happiness or associate happiness with in this temporary life. Happiness is usually defined in terms of presence, here and now. It may be associated with bodily pleasure which is always short-lived. In a consumerist world, it is associated with material wealth that is elusive, and when it seems to be attained, either wealth leaves one, or one leaves it. The very act of buying and hoarding things may be misconstrued as happiness. And the very notion of chasing a life that is loaded with fun is a futile effort, for no fun activity can be maintained. This is why people escape into addictions of all sorts, including drugs and alcohol. Life entails at least some seriousness.

In comedy, the protagonist moves from a tragic or sad beginning to a 'happy' ending. In tragedy, the protagonist begins with some kind of a 'happy' life but ends up miserable. In both cases, the beginning and end are here and now, in this life. There is no link to the Hereafter, a notion that seems to have disappeared from contemporary narratives.

It is different when one is conscious about the Hereafter, and invests in this life what shall be reaped in the Hereafter in the form of eternal happiness. Wealth is acquired and spent in a way that pleases Allah. Hardships are endured and difficulties tolerated because ultimately everything comes from Allah. Pleasure is in moderation in ways that please Allah. Everything is done with an eye on the next world, where happiness is wholesome and eternal.

It is recognising that grace has potentially two ways in one's relationship with anyone. Grace manifests itself by coming one's way like the knowledge of Allah, and it is grace to impart this knowledge in return to others. This is happiness that paves the way to eternal felicity.

20

A Plantation for the Hereafter

وَقَدْ عَلِمَ أَرْبَابُ القُلُوبِ أَنَّ الدُّنْيَا مَزْرَعَةُ الآخِرَةِ، والقَلْبُ
كَالأَرْضِ، والإِيمَانُ كَالبَذْرِ فِيهِ، والطَّاعَاتُ جَارِيَةٌ مَجْرَى
تَقَلُّبِ الأَرْضِ وَتَطْهِيرِهَا وَمَجْرَى حَفْرِ الأَنْهَارِ وَسِيَاقَةِ المَاءِ
إِلَيْهَا، والقَلْبُ المُسْتَهْتِرُ بِالدُّنْيَا المُسْتَغْرِقُ بِهَا كَالأَرْضِ السَّبْخَةِ
الَّتِي لَا يَنْمُو فِيهَا البَذْرُ وَيَوْمُ القِيَامَةِ يَوْمُ الحَصَادِ، لَا يَحْصُدُ
أَحَدٌ إِلَّا مَا زَرَعَ، وَلَا يَنْمُو زَرْعٌ إِلَّا مِنْ بَذْرِ الإِيمَانِ، وَقَلَّمَا
يَنْفَعُ إِيمَانٌ مَعَ خُبْثِ القَلْبِ وَسُوءِ أَخْلَاقِهِ، كَمَا لَا يَنْمُو بَذْرٌ فِي
سَبْخَةٍ، فَيَنْبَغِي أَنْ يُقَاسَ رَجَاءُ العَبْدِ المَغْفِرَةَ بِرَجَاءِ صَاحِبِ
الزَّرْعِ، فَكُلُّ مَنْ طَلَبَ أَرْضاً طَيِّبَةً وَأَلْقَى فِيهَا بَذْراً جَيِّداً غَيْرَ
عَفِنٍ وَلَا مُسَوَّسٍ، ثُمَّ أَمَدَّهُ بِمَا يَحْتَاجُ إِلَيْهِ وَهُوَ سَوْقُ المَاءِ إِلَيْهِ
فِي أَوْقَاتِهِ، ثُمَّ نَفَى الشَّوْكَ عَنِ الأَرْضِ والحَشِيشِ وَكُلَّ مَا يَمْنَعُ

نَبَاتَ البَذْرِ أَوْ يُفْسِدُهُ، ثُمَّ جَلَسَ مُنْتَظِراً مِنْ فَضْلِ اللهِ تَعَالَى

دَفْعَ الصَّوَاعِقِ وَالآفَاتِ المُفْسِدَةِ إِلَى أَنْ يَتِمَّ الزَّرْعُ وَيَبْلُغَ غَايَتَهُ:

سُمِّيَ انْتِظَارُهُ رَجَاءً. وَإِنْ بُثَّ البَذْرُ فِي أَرْضٍ صُلْبَةٍ سَبْخَةٍ

مُرْتَفِعَةٍ لَا يَنْصَبُّ إِلَيْهَا المَاءُ وَلَمْ يَشْتَغِلْ بِتَعَهُّدِ البَذْرِ أَصْلاً، ثُمَّ

انْتَظَرَ الحَصَادَ مِنْهُ: سُمِّيَ انْتِظَارُهُ حُمْقاً وَغُرُوراً لَا رَجَاءً. وَإِنْ

بُثَّ البَذْرُ فِي أَرْضٍ طَيِّبَةٍ وَلَكِنْ لَا مَاءَ لَهَا وَأَخَذَ يَنْتَظِرُ مِيَاهَ

الأَمْطَارِ حَيْثُ لَا تَغْلِبُ الأَمْطَارُ وَلَا تُمْتَنَعُ أَيْضاً: سُمِّيَ

انْتِظَارُهُ تَمَنِّياً لَا رَجَاءً.[20]

The masters of the hearts knew that this world is a
plantation for the Hereafter and that the heart is like
the soil, and faith is like sowing seeds in it, and acts of
obedience are like tilling the land and clearing it, and
digging waterways to bring water to it. As for the heart
that is careless about this world while being absorbed in
it, it is like a salt swamp where seeds do not grow. On
the Day of Judgment, the day of harvesting, each will
harvest what he had planted, where no plant will grow
except for the one who sowed the seeds of faith. Hardly
does faith benefit while the heart is impure and one's
character traits are bad, just as seeds do not grow in a
salt swamp. The servant's hope for forgiveness should
be analogous to the hope of the farmer. He who seeks a
fertile land and sows good seeds that are neither rotten
nor infested, and supplies it with what it needs, which

---

20. Al-Ghazālī, *Iḥyā' ʿUlūm al-Dīn*, edited by Sulaymān Dunyā, Beirut: Dār al-Maʿrifah, p. 143.

is irrigation at specified times, and performs weeding, removing thorns and grass and all that prevents the seeds from growing or destroying them, and 'he sits down' waiting for the favour of Allah Most High to keep away thunderbolts and corrupting diseases until the plants are mature (or ripe) and reach their purpose, then his waiting is called *hope*. But if he spreads the seeds in a high salty swamp, where water does not reach, and does not even attempt to care for the seeds, and then he waits for the harvest, his waiting is called *stupidity* and *delusion*, not hope. And if he sows the seeds on fertile land that lacks water and waits for rain where there is not much rain, but also rain is not ruled out/impossible, then his waiting is called *wishful thinking*, not hope.

There are two kinds of hearts. One heart is like a fertile land where planting is very promising and it is logical to be hopeful and anticipate good crops, if one tills the land and cares for it. If one fails to irrigate the plants or nurture them, even when the land is fertile, it is considered wishful thinking to expect any good harvest. The other heart is like salty marshland whereby it is sheer stupidity to even think of planting anything there, for this goes against the very nature of things.

Every human heart is a good and fertile land at the moment of birth. All children remain in that state until their parents and the social environment start to corrupt the goodness inherited in their hearts. But a fertile land does not help that much if the seeds themselves are rotten. Decaying seeds may be likened to immoral or ungodly thoughts that one might accommodate in one's heart in violation of the good natural disposition, with which one was born. The good seeds of moral behaviour are to be found in the Holy Qur'ān and the Prophetic Sunnah as well as in obedience of Allah, performing good deeds and continuous cleansing of the heart with remembrance of the name of Allah. The heart is the field where one sows seeds in this life, while the harvest is reaped in the Hereafter.

The Qur'ān reminds humanity about the true nature of this life through the metaphor of the different phases of plant development: *Know that the life of this world is but amusement and diversion and adornment and boasting to one another and competition in increase of wealth and children – like the example of a rain whose [resulting] plant growth pleases the tillers; then it dries and you see it turned yellow; then it becomes [scattered] debris. And in the Hereafter is severe punishment and forgiveness from Allah and approval. And what is the worldly life except the enjoyment of delusion?* (Qur'ān 57:20)

Those who positively seek forgiveness should be like the farmer who sows healthy plants (good deeds) and weeds them (prevents sins from interrupting his plan).

21

Shamefully Busy

وَاعْلَمْ أَنَّ الزُّهْدَ دَرَجَةٌ هِيَ كَمَالُ الْأَبْرَارِ وَصَاحِبُ هذِهِ الْحَالَةِ
مِنَ الْمُقَرَّبِينَ، فَلَا جَرَمَ صَارَ الزُّهْدُ فِي حَقِّهِ نُقْصَانًا، إِذْ حَسَنَاتُ
الْأَبْرَارِ سَيِّئَاتُ الْمُقَرَّبِينَ، وَهذَا الْآنَ الْكَارِهُ لِلدُّنْيَا مَشْغُولٌ
بِالدُّنْيَا، كَمَا أَنَّ الرَّاغِبَ فِيهَا مَشْغُولٌ بِهَا، وَالشُّغْلُ بِمَا سِوَى اللهِ
تَعَالَى حِجَابٌ عَنِ اللهِ تَعَالَى، إِذْ لَا بُعْدَ بَيْنَكَ وَبَيْنَ اللهِ تَعَالَى
حَتَّى يَكُونَ الْبُعْدُ حِجَابًا، فَإِنَّهُ أَقْرَبُ إِلَيْكَ مِنْ حَبْلِ الْوَرِيدِ،
وَلَيْسَ هُوَ فِي مَكَانٍ حَتَّى تَكُونَ السَّمَاوَاتُ وَالْأَرْضُ حِجَابًا
بَيْنَكَ وَبَيْنَهُ، فَلَا حِجَابَ بَيْنَكَ وَبَيْنَهُ إِلَّا شُغْلُكَ بِغَيْرِهِ، وَشُغْلُكَ
بِنَفْسِكَ وَشَهَوَاتِكَ شُغْلٌ بِغَيْرِهِ، وَأَنْتَ لَا تَزَالُ مَشْغُولًا بِنَفْسِكَ
وَشَهَوَاتِ نَفْسِكَ فَكَذَلِكَ لَا تَزَالُ مَحْجُوبًا عَنْهُ، فَالْمَشْغُولُ
بِحُبِّ نَفْسِهِ مَشْغُولٌ عَنِ اللهِ تَعَالَى، وَالْمَشْغُولُ بِبُغْضِ نَفْسِهِ
أَيْضًا مَشْغُولٌ عَنِ اللهِ تَعَالَى بِكُلِّ مَا سِوَى اللهِ.[21]

---

21. Al-Ghazālī, *Iḥyā' ʿUlūm al-Dīn*, edited by Sulaymān Dunyā, Beirut: Dār al-Maʿrifah, p. 3.

Know that asceticism is a rank which is the perfection of the righteous people, and the possessor of this state is among those who are drawn near [to Allah]. There is no doubt, then, that asceticism is considered a shortcoming in the latter's case, for the good deeds of the righteous are the bad deeds of those drawn near. This is so because the one who hates this world is one who is preoccupied with it, just as the one who desires it is preoccupied with it, and to be preoccupied with something other than Allah Most High is a veil from Him, for there is no distance between you and Allah Most High so that the distance would become an obstacle, for He is closer to you than your jugular vein, nor does He exist in a place so that the earth and the heavens would form a veil between you and Him. There is no veil between you and Him except that you are busy with other things than Him, and being busy with yourself and your lusts is being busy with other than Him, and as long as you are busy with yourself and your lusts you will still be veiled from Him, and the one who is busy with self-love is distracted from Allah Most High, and the one who hates himself is also distracted from Allah Most High, being busy as he is with everything other than Allah.

*A*nd *We have already created man and know what his soul whispers to him, and We are closer to him than [his] jugular vein.* (Qur'ān 50:16)

Allah Most High is very close to us, not in a spatial relationship, because He does not exist in space and time. We are always present in His knowledge, but the problem is that we might not choose to be with Him all the time. We get distracted with mundane things. We get distracted with the dictates of our egos. What a loss when those who disdain materialism and those who are obsessed with it are both busy with this world! Any concern that is not for the sake of Allah is a veil. This is why asceticism, which is essentially a detachment from this world, brings the servant to Allah. It perfects his character traits to the extent that worldliness is shunned, for being conscious of worldly affairs distances one from Allah.

Our lusts and desires are obstacles that distract us from Him. There are amongst us those who love themselves, with various degrees of narcissism which manifests itself through the big 'I', only 'I', an obsession with selfies and social media that focuses on one's image, with no content that serves public good. These are, in their estimation, at the centre of the world. And there are those who are not happy with themselves, unlike their narcissistic counterparts. The problem with both is that they do not see that vast universe of wonderful signs that points in the direction of the Divine all the time. For those who 'love' and those who 'hate' inappropriately, they need to liberate themselves from these veils. They need to accept themselves for what they really are and move closer to the Creator of this existence.

22

Sins as True Veils

اِعْلَمْ أَنَّ التَّوْبَةَ عِبَارَةٌ عَنْ مَعْنًى يَنْتَظِمُ وَيَلْتَئِمُ مِنْ ثَلَاثَةِ أُمُورٍ مُرَتَّبَةٍ: عِلْمٌ، وَحَالٌ، وَفِعْلٌ. فَالعِلْمُ الأَوَّلُ والحَالُ الثَّانِي، والفِعْلُ الثَّالِثُ. والأَوَّلُ مُوجِبٌ لِلثَّانِي، والثَّانِي مُوجِبٌ لِلثَّالِثِ إِيجَابًا اقْتَضَاهُ اطِّرَادُ سُنَّةِ اللهِ فِي المُلْكِ والمَلَكُوتِ. أَمَّا العِلْمُ فَهُوَ مَعْرِفَةُ عِظَمِ ضَرَرِ الذُّنُوبِ وَكَوْنِهَا حِجَابًا بَيْنَ العَبْدِ وَبَيْنَ كُلِّ مَحْبُوبٍ، فَإِذَا عَرَفْتَ ذَلِكَ مَعْرِفَةً مُحَقَّقَةً بِيَقِينٍ غَالِبٍ عَلَى قَلْبِكَ ثَارَ مِنْ هَذِهِ المَعْرِفَةِ تَأَلُّمٌ لِلْقَلْبِ بِسَبَبِ فَوَاتِ المَحْبُوبِ، فَإِنَّ لِلْقَلْبِ مَهْمَا شَعَرَ بِفَوَاتِ مَحْبُوبِهِ تَأَلَّمَ، فَإِنْ كَانَ فَوَاتُهُ بِفِعْلِهِ تَأَسَّفَ عَلَى الفِعْلِ المُفَوِّتِ، فَيُسَمَّى تَأَلُّمُهُ بِسَبَبِ فِعْلِهِ المُفَوِّتِ لِمَحْبُوبِهِ نَدَمًا. فَإِذَا غَلَبَ هَذَا الأَلَمُ عَلَى القَلْبِ واسْتَوْلَى وانْبَعَثَ مِنْ هَذَا الأَلَمِ فِي القَلْبِ حَالَةٌ أُخْرَى تُسَمَّى إِرَادَةً وقَصْدًا إِلَى فِعْلٍ تَعَلَّقَ بِالحَالِ والمَاضِي وَبِالاسْتِقْبَالِ، أَمَّا تَعَلُّقُهُ بِالحَالِ فَبِالتَّرْكِ لِلذَّنْبِ الذِي كَانَ مُلَابِسًا، وأَمَّا بِالاسْتِقْبَالِ فَبِالعَزْمِ عَلَى

تَرْكِ الذَّنْبِ المَفُوتِ لِلْمَحُبُوبِ إِلَى آخِرِ العُمْرِ، وَأَمَّا بِالمَاضِي
فَتِلَاقِي مَا فَاتَ بِالجَبْرِ وَالقَضَاءِ إِنْ كَانَ قَابِلاً لِلجَبْرِ.[22]

Know that repentance is tantamount to a meaning that
is organised and brought together by three orderly
components: knowledge, state and action. Knowledge
comes first, state comes second and then action comes
third. The first is a requisite of the second, and the
second is a requisite of the third, an imperative requisite
dictated by the repetition of Allah's norm in the physical
and spiritual worlds. As for knowledge, it is to realise
the great harm of sins, and that they form a veil between
the servant and every beloved. If you realise this
through experiential knowledge by way of a certitude
that prevails over your heart, there ensues from this
knowledge a pain in the heart because of missing the
beloved. Indeed, the heart experiences pain for as long
as it feels the loss of the beloved. If the loss is the result
of its own action, it would be sorry for the action that
led to the loss, and the pain felt over the action that led
to the loss of the beloved is called *regret*. If the pain in
the heart becomes overwhelming and prevalent, then
out of this pain springs in the heart another state called
'will' and 'motivation' toward an action pertaining to the
present, the past and the future. As for the present, it is
abandoning the sin that it was entrapped in; as for the
future, it is having the intention to stay away from the
sin that caused the loss of the beloved until the end of
its life; and as for the past, it is attempting to repair
and make up what was lost, if it can be repaired.

---

22. Al-Ghazālī, *Iḥyā' 'Ulūm al-Dīn*, edited by Sulaymān Dunyā,
Beirut: Dār al-Maʿrifah, p. 191.

*I*nstead of drifting away from the Islamic worldview and committing sin, it is possible to rectify one's path and return to Allah Who is the Forgiver. Repentance is between the human being and Allah, with no one in between. There is no confession and no absolution which takes place at the hand of another person. Only Allah may forgive sins, including grave sins, and to Him only should one direct one's supplications and ask for forgiveness. One is also forbidden from publicising one's sins.

Repentance entails knowledge, a state of heart and an action, in the order mentioned. The first is to know that sin is the reason for the loss of the beloved. Our sins trap us, keep us veiled from the truth and prevent us from seeing the great harm that sins inflict on us. We need to realise the negative impact of sinning on our wellbeing, and that a sin can be short-lived, but it leaves a bitter taste for a lifetime. It has been said: 'O [sinful] pleasure that is no more! O heart-breaking remorse that remains evermore!' A moment of sinful and illicit sexual pleasure may be associated with a lack of commitment, loyalty or true love. But sin can also be an act of transgression which violates the sanctity of life, an act of racism that undermines the dignity of the human being, or an act of theft of property or colonisation of a country. Once the full scope of sin is displayed before our consciences, its damage manifesting itself, and one recognises the distance created between one and the beloved, then the heart agonises and twists and turns in pain over defying the Divine order.

The following verse lists the advantages of repentance and forsaking sins for the benefit of the whole community: *And [Noah] said, 'Ask forgiveness of your Lord. Indeed, He is ever a Perpetual Forgiver. He will send [rain from] the sky upon you in [continuing] showers. And give you increase in wealth and children and provide for you gardens and provide for you rivers.'* (Qur'ān 71:10-12) Certain sins that include material damage to fellow human beings, such as theft, entails that repentance should include restitution of the material damage or compensation.

23

Occasionalism (Allah Is the Cause of all Events)

أَنْ يَنْكَشِفَ لَكَ أَنْ لَا فَاعِلَ إِلَّا اللهُ تَعَالَى، وَأَنَّ كُلَّ مَوْجُودٍ مِنْ
خَلْقٍ وَرِزْقٍ وَعَطَاءٍ وَمَنْعٍ وَحَيَاةٍ وَمَوْتٍ وَغِنَّى وَفَقْرٍ إِلَى غَيْرِ
ذَلِكَ مِمَّا يَنْطَلِقُ عَلَيْهِ اسْمٌ فَالْمُنْفَرِدُ بِإِبْدَاعِهِ وَاخْتِرَاعِهِ هُوَ اللهُ
عَزَّ وَجَلَّ لَا شَرِيكَ لَهُ فِيهِ، وَإِذَا انْكَشَفَ لَكَ هَذَا لَمْ تَنْظُرْ إِلَى
غَيْرِهِ، بَلْ كَانَ مِنْهُ خَوْفُكَ وَإِلَيْهِ رَجَاؤُكَ وَبِهِ ثِقَتُكَ وَعَلَيْهِ
اتِّكَالُكَ، فَإِنَّهُ الْفَاعِلُ عَلَى الِانْفِرَادِ دُونَ غَيْرِهِ، وَمَا سِوَاهُ
مُسَخَّرُونَ لَا اسْتِقْلَالَ لَهُمْ بِتَحْرِيكِ ذَرَّةٍ مِنْ مَلَكُوتِ
السَّمَوَاتِ وَالْأَرْضِ. [23]

That it will be unveiled to you that there is no real
doer except Allah Most High, and that every existent,
whether a created being, a sustenance, a bestowal or

---

23.   Al-Ghazālī, *Iḥyā' ʿUlūm al-Dīn*, edited by Sulaymān Dunyā,
Beirut: Dār al-Maʿrifah, p. 247.

withholding, life or death, wealth or poverty, and everything else that can be named, the one and only one that
has made and created it is Allah, glorified and exalted
is He, with no other partners. When this is unveiled
to you, you will not look at anyone other than Him.
Rather, your fear shall be of Him and your hope shall
be in Him, your trust and reliance shall be in Him, for
He is the unique doer and no one else does anything
apart from Him, and everyone else is subjected to His
will, not having independence to move one atom in
the domains of the heavens and earth.

*A*l-Ghazālī's statement that Allah Most High is the
real cause of every action or phenomenon in the
universe is called occasionalism. He is the Creator
and Sustainer of this universe which He continues to
recreate at every instant. This requires a unique relationship with Allah based on being indebted to Him
for everything, for everything is in His hands. If there
is one phrase that characterises the calling of all the
prophets of Allah in the Qur'ān, it is the call: *O my
people, worship Allah; you have no deity other than
Him.* (Qur'ān 7:65; 23:23; 11:50)

The theological cornerstone of Islam is *tawḥīd*,
which includes believing in the oneness of Allah,
taking as Lord no other deity other than Him, no
other persons or objects that share His attributes,
for *nothing is like unto Him.* (Qur'ān 42:11) He
is other than all that He has created, and He,

therefore, cannot be bound by space and time. No representation, two or three-dimensional, is possible in His respect, and all the paintings, statues and idols that purport represent Him are antithetical to His nature. All people who speak Arabic use the word 'Allah' in reference to God, including the Christian Arabs in their mass or service. But while in Islam the *oneness* of Allah requires a clear distinction between Allah, the Spirit of the Holy (i.e., the archangel Gabriel), and Jesus Christ (the Word of Allah to Mary and a prophet of Islam), Christians developed a Trinitarian theology, a post-revelational construct, where 'in the *unity* of the Godhead there are three persons, the Father, the Son, and the Holy Spirit.' The Qur'ān responds to the above historical theological development as follows: *O People of the Scripture, do not commit excess in your religion or say anything about Allah but the truth. The Messiah, Jesus, the son of Mary, was but a messenger of Allah and His word which He directed to Mary and a soul [created at a command] from Him. So believe in Allah and His messengers. And do not say, 'Three'; desist – it is better for you. Indeed, Allah is but one God. Exalted is He above having a son...* (Qur'ān 4:171)

Love Is the Renewed
Imperative

اِعْلَمْ أَنَّ الأُمَّةَ مُجْمَعَةٌ عَلَى أَنَّ الحُبَّ لِلهِ تَعَالَى وَلِرَسُولِهِ صَلَّى
اللهُ عَلَيْهِ وَسَلَّمَ فَرْضٌ، وَكَيْفَ يُفْرَضُ مَا لَا وُجُودَ لَهُ وَكَيْفَ
يُفَسَّرُ الحُبُّ بِالطَّاعَةِ وَالطَّاعَةُ تَبَعُ الحُبِّ وَثَمَرَتُهُ؟ فَلَابُدَّ وَأَنْ
يَتَقَدَّمَ الحُبُّ ثُمَّ بَعْدَ ذَلِكَ يُطِيعُ مَنْ أَحَبَّ. وَيَدُلُّ عَلَى إِثْبَاتِ
الحُبِّ لِلهِ تَعَالَى قَوْلُهُ عَزَّ وَجَلَّ: يَا أَيُّهَا الَّذِينَ آمَنُوا مَنْ يَرْتَدَّ
مِنكُمْ عَنْ دِينِهِ فَسَوْفَ يَأْتِي اللهُ بِقَوْمٍ يُحِبُّهُمْ وَيُحِبُّونَهُ أَذِلَّةٍ عَلَى
الْمُؤْمِنِينَ أَعِزَّةٍ عَلَى الْكَافِرِينَ يُجَاهِدُونَ فِي سَبِيلِ اللهِ
وَلَا يَخَافُونَ لَوْمَةَ لَائِمٍ ذَلِكَ فَضْلُ اللهِ يُؤْتِيهِ مَن يَشَاءُ
وَاللهُ وَاسِعٌ عَلِيمٌ (المائدة:٥٤) وقوله تعالى: وَمِنَ النَّاسِ مَن
يَتَّخِذُ مِنْ دُونِ اللهِ أَندَادًا يُحِبُّونَهُمْ كَحُبِّ اللهِ وَالَّذِينَ آمَنُوا

أَشَدُّ حُبًّا لِلهِ (البقرة:١٦٥) وَهُوَ دَلِيلٌ عَلَى إِثْبَاتِ الحُبِّ
وَإِثْبَاتِ التَّفَاوُتِ فِيهِ.[24]

Know that the Muslim *Ummah* is unanimous that love for Allah Most High and for His Messenger ﷺ is an obligation, for how could something be made imperative if it were non-existent? And how to explain love as meaning obedience when obedience is subsequent to love and is its fruit? Love must come first and then one obeys one whom one loves. The proof for the affirmation of the love of Allah Most High is found in the words of Allah, exalted is He, *O believers, whosoever of you turns from his religion, God will assuredly bring a people He loves, and who love Him, humble towards the believers, disdainful towards the unbelievers, men who struggle in the path of God, not fearing the reproach of any reproacher. That is God's bounty; He gives it unto whom He will; and God is All-embracing, All-knowing* [al-Mā'idah: 54], and His words, *Yet there be men who take to themselves compeers apart from God, loving them as God is loved; but those that believe love God more ardently* [al-Baqarah: 165]. This is an evidence for the affirmation of love and its disparity amongst people.

The first article of faith is to believe in Allah, believing that He is unique and distinct from creation, and

---

24. Al-Ghazālī, *Iḥyā' 'Ulūm al-Dīn*, edited by Sulaymān Dunyā, Beirut: Dār al-Ma'rifah, p. 294.

believing in all His Most Beautiful Names. But above all, love of Allah comes first, and one is invited to reach this level of closeness to Him. The criterion for this love is trying to live according to His revealed message to the best of one's ability by following the Prophetic model: *Say, [O Muhammad], 'If you should love Allah, then follow me, [so] Allah will love you and forgive you your sins. And Allah is Forgiving and Merciful.'* (Qur'ān 3:31)

Love entails following the one one loves as an expression of love itself. If I love the Prophet ﷺ, then I will certainly express my love through following his example, for what good is it to claim to love him and lead a life that contradicts his way? Indeed, Divine love translates into loving the Prophet ﷺ. In *Love in the Holy Qur'an*, HRH Prince Ghazi bin Muhammad writes: 'A person's love of God requires – and inevitably leads to – love of what reminds him or her of God, and this means loving the Messenger.' He then lists loving religion, prayers, and nature among other things.[25] Those who are true believers are more passionate in their love of Allah. Love in this case is the highest expression of obedience. Those who turn away from Allah and become disbelievers will be substituted with those whom Allah loves and they love Him. He initiates love and they respond

---

25. Ghazi bin Muhammad, *Love in the Holy Qur'an* (Kazi Publications: Chicago, 2010) English translation of 6th Arabic edition, p. 104.

with love: *O you who have believed, whoever of you should revert from his religion – Allah will bring forth [in place of them] a people He will love and who will love Him ...* (Qur'ān 5:54)

Love has a salvific value. The Prophet ﷺ told a Bedouin who loves Allah and His Messenger, but prepared little else for the Hereafter, that a person will be with the one he loves.[26]

---

26. Aḥmad Ibn Ḥanbal's *Musnad*. ḥadīth of Anas ibn Mālik. (Summary)

On Knowledge, Action and Sincerity

أَمَّا بَعُدُ: فَقَدِ انْكَشَفَ لِأَرْبَابِ القُلُوبِ بِبَصِيرَةِ الإِيمَانِ وَأَنْوَارِ
القُرْآنِ أَنْ لَا وُصُولَ إِلَى السَّعَادَةِ إِلَّا بِالعِلْمِ وَالعِبَادَةِ، فَالنَّاسُ
كُلُّهُمْ هَلْكَى إِلَّا العَالِمُونَ، وَالعَالِمُونَ كُلُّهُمْ هَلْكَى
إِلَّا العَامِلُونَ، وَالعَامِلُونَ كُلُّهُمْ هَلْكَى إِلَّا المُخْلِصُونَ،
وَالمُخْلِصُونَ عَلَى خَطَرٍ عَظِيمٍ. فَالعَمَلُ بِغَيْرِ نِيَّةٍ عَنَاءٌ، وَالنِّيَّةُ
بِغَيْرِ إِخْلَاصٍ رِيَاءٌ، وَهُوَ لِلتَّقَاءِ، وَمَعَ العِصْيَانِ سَوَاءٌ، وَالإِخْلَاصُ
مِنْ غَيْرِ صِدْقٍ تَحْقِيقٌ هَبَاءٌ، وَقَدْ قَالَ اللهُ تَعَالَى فِي كُلِّ عَمَلٍ
كَانَ بِإِرَادَةِ غَيْرِ اللهِ مَشُوبًا مَغْمُورًا. قَالَ تَعَالَى: ﴿وَقَدِمْنَا إِلَى
مَا عَمِلُوا مِنْ عَمَلٍ فَجَعَلْنَاهُ هَبَاءً مَنْثُورًا﴾ (الفُرْقَان: ٢٣).[27]

---

27. Al-Ghazālī, *Iḥyā' ʿUlūm al-Dīn*, edited by Sulaymān Dunyā, Beirut: Dār al-Maʿrifah, p. 362.

It has been revealed to the masters of the hearts, through the insight of faith and the lights of the Qur'ān, that there is no way to happiness except through knowledge and worship, for all people are doomed except for those who have knowledge, and those who have knowledge are doomed except for those who act on it, and those who act on it are doomed except for those who are sincere, and the sincere face great danger. Indeed, work without intention is nothing but toil, and intention without sincerity is showing off, which is the equivalent of being two-faced, and it is the same as disobedience, and sincerity without true realisation is like dust. Allah Most High said about every impure deed not done for His sake: *And We will regard what they have done of deeds and make them as dust dispersed.* (Qur'ān 25:23)

*T*he path to happiness is paved with a combination of true knowledge, right action, good intention and pure sincerity. Knowledge without action is a theoretical stage, and it may amount to nothing in the scales of the Hereafter, such as knowing that backbiting is prohibited but continuing nevertheless to engage in this grave sin.

The ultimate purpose of creation is to worship Allah which is first and foremost reflected in action as in the five daily prayers or the Pilgrimage to Makkah. Action may include recollecting the name of Allah, supplication or simply pondering on the universe. All those who have consciousness are required to worship the Almighty:

And I did not create the jinn and mankind except to worship Me. (Qur'ān 51:56)

On the other hand, action without knowledge can lead to disaster. Fasting is imperative for all adult Muslims under normal circumstances. Not knowing that it is acceptable not to fast during the month of Ramadan for the terminally ill and still fasting may have dire health consequences. One can only imagine a host of other issues, including the status of women and non-Muslims, where the lack of adequate knowledge may lead to unfortunate results.

Action should furthermore be appropriate, as the two extremes of excess and deficiency should be avoided. The story of the three Companions who convinced themselves to go to extremes in their spiritual life is an excellent example of inappropriate action, even when it is done in the area of spirituality. One of them pledged to fast every day of his life, the second one committed himself to praying throughout the night, every night of his life, and the last one wanted to be celibate. Upon knowing about their intentions, the Prophet ﷺ stated that his way of life includes fasting, but also not fasting (i.e. in other than Ramadan), praying at night but also sleeping, and that getting married is his Prophetic example.

Even when done the right way, technically, action needs sincerity and the right intention for it to be accepted. It cannot be done for the sake of other than Allah.

There Are Absolutely No Secrets

اعْلَمْ أَنَّ حَقِيقَةَ المُرَاقَبَةِ هِيَ مُلَاحَظَةُ الرَّقِيبِ وانْصِرافُ الهَمِّ
إِلَيْهِ، فَمَنِ احْتَرَزَ مِنْ أَمْرٍ مِنَ الأُمُورِ بِسَبَبِ غَيْرِهِ يُقَالُ إِنَّهُ يُرَاقِبُ
فُلَاناً وَيُرَاعِي جَانِبَهُ، وَيَعْنِي بِهَذِهِ المُرَاقَبَةِ حَالَةً لِلْقَلْبِ يُثْمِرُها
نَوْعٌ مِنَ المَعْرِفَةِ، وَتُثْمِرُ تِلْكَ الحَالَةُ أَعْمَالاً فِي الجَوَارِحِ
وَ فِي القَلْبِ. أَمَّا الحَالَةُ فَهِيَ مُرَاعَاةُ القَلْبِ لِلرَّقِيبِ واشْتِغَالُهُ
بِهِ والْتِفَاتُهُ إِلَيْهِ وَمُلَاحَظَتُهُ إِيَّاهُ وانْصِرافُهُ إِلَيْهِ. وأمَّا المَعْرِفَةُ
الَّتِي تُثْمِرُ هَذِهِ الحَالَةَ فَهِيَ العِلْمُ بِأَنَّ اللهَ مُطَّلِعٌ عَلَى الضَّمَائِرِ عَالِمٌ
بِالسَّرَائِرِ رَقِيبٌ عَلَى أَعْمَالِ العِبَادِ قَائِمٌ عَلَىٰ كُلِّ نَفْسٍ بِمَا كَسَبَتْ،
وأنَّ سِرَّ القَلْبِ فِي حَقِّهِ مَكْشُوفٌ كَمَا أَنَّ ظَاهِرَ البَشَرَةِ
لِلْخَلْقِ مَكْشُوفٌ بَلْ أَشَدِّ مِنْ ذَلِكَ.[28]

---

28. Al-Ghazālī, *Iḥyā' ʿUlūm al-Dīn*, edited by Sulaymān Dunyā, Beirut: Dār al-Maʿrifah, p. 398.

Know that the reality of watchfulness is observing Him
who is ever watchful and devoting all one's concern
to him. It is said: the person who refrains from doing
something because of someone else is watching so-and-so
and takes him into consideration. By this watchfulness
is meant a state of the heart which is the fruit of a kind
of knowledge, and this state yields outward action
and also works of the heart. As for the state, it is the
heart's observance of the one who is watching, its
preoccupation with him, its inclination towards him, its
observation of him and its being entirely focused on him.
The knowledge that brings to fruition this state is the
realisation that Allah sees what is in people's consciences,
that He knows people's hidden secrets, that He watches
over people's deeds, that He holds every soul accountable
for what it has earned, and that the secret of the heart
is revealed to Him, just as the skin is exposed to other
people, indeed, if not much more than that.

*T*here is naught in this universe except that it is known
to Allah, even thoughts and ideas. Whatever crosses
one's mind is known to Him; one may keep 'secrets'
from other people but one can never keep anything
hidden from Allah: *And conceal your speech or
publicise it; indeed, He is Knowing of that within the
breasts.* (Qur'ān 67:13) Allah knows all that takes
place in the universe at once, for He is Omniscient.
This attribute is part and parcel of the Islamic
creed. The awareness of this attribute, that we are
constantly exposed to Him, should have a positive

impact on our behaviour. One should be embarrassed to harbour ill thoughts or ill feelings in one's heart or to contemplate wrongdoing, being fully aware that Allah continuously watches one. Moving from being watched to the Watchful, Allah, one should check the action that one contemplates; if it is for His sake, then it should be carried out, but if it is for the sake of Satan, one should refrain immediately from it. And when an action is done for Allah's sake, it should be perfected, taking into consideration all the proper proprieties associated with it.

Being conscious of the exposure of the heart leads to the modification of one's behaviour, hastening to do what is right in the sight of Allah, and shunning what He has prohibited. The heart will then be tranquil, and the limbs will be the witnesses to this state of the heart, by partaking in its tranquillity. As Allah knows one's best kept secrets, including sinful deeds that are known only to him, one should ask for forgiveness and protection against ill intentions as well as against being exposed in public.

One usually makes one's appearance good for others to see, because they can be seen, and only when one's appearance are seen by them. The same logic applies to the heart. It is seen by Allah all the time. Therefore, one should make one's heart good for Him, by cleansing it from all impurities and adorning it with His traits.

27

Thinking and Having a Preference for the Eternal

اِعْلَمْ أَنَّ مَعْنَى الْفِكْرِ هُوَ إِحْضَارُ مَعْرِفَتَيْنِ فِي الْقَلْبِ لِيَسْتَثْمِرَ مِنْهُمَا مَعْرِفَةً ثَالِثَةً. وَمِثَالُهُ أَنَّ مَنْ مَالَ إِلَى الْعَاجِلَةِ وَآثَرَ الْحَيَاةَ الدُّنْيَا وَأَرَادَ أَنْ يَعْرِفَ أَنَّ الْآخِرَةَ أَوْلَى بِالْإِيثَارِ مِنَ الْعَاجِلَةِ فَلَهُ طَرِيقَانِ (أَحَدُهُمَا) أَنْ يَسْمَعَ مِنْ غَيْرِهِ أَنَّ الْآخِرَةَ أَوْلَى بِالْإِيثَارِ مِنَ الدُّنْيَا، فَيُقَلِّدَهُ وَيُصَدِّقَهُ مِنْ غَيْرِ بَصِيرَةٍ بِحَقِيقَةِ الْأَمْرِ فَيَمِيلُ بِعَمَلِهِ إِلَى إِيثَارِ الْآخِرَةِ اعْتِمَاداً عَلَى مُجَرَّدِ قَوْلِهِ، وَهَذَا يُسَمَّى تَقْلِيداً وَلَا يُسَمَّى مَعْرِفَةً. (وَالطَّرِيقُ الثَّانِي) أَنْ يَعْرِفَ أَنَّ الْأَبْقَى أَوْلَى بِالْإِيثَارِ، ثُمَّ يَعْرِفَ أَنَّ الْآخِرَةَ أَبْقَى. فَيَحْصُلُ لَهُ مِنْ هَاتَيْنِ الْمَعْرِفَتَيْنِ مَعْرِفَةٌ ثَالِثَةٌ وَهُوَ أَنَّ الْآخِرَةَ أَوْلَى بِالْإِيثَارِ

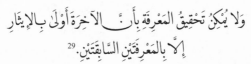

وَلَا يُمْكِنُ تَحْقِيقُ المَعْرِفَةِ بِأَنَّ الآخِرَةَ أَوْلَى بِالإِيثَارِ
إِلَّا بِالمَعْرِفَتَيْنِ السَّابِقَتَيْنِ.[29]

Know that the meaning of ratiocination is summoning
two known notions in the heart in order to extract from
them a third notion. For instance, if a person who is
inclined to the evanescent world and prefers this earthly
life wanted to know that the Hereafter has a better
right to be preferred, then there are two ways for him
to know this. One is that he hears from someone else
that the Hereafter has a better right to be preferable,
and thereafter he imitates him and believes him without
having an insight into the reality of things, hence
becoming inclined to prefer the Hereafter exclusively
on the basis of his mere statement, and this is called
imitation, not knowledge. The second is to know that
what is everlasting has a better right to be preferred
and that the Hereafter is everlasting, then he draws
from these two ideas a third one which is that the
Hereafter has a better right to be preferred. And it is
not possible to discern the knowledge that the Hereafter
has a better right to be preferred except through the
previous two ideas.

*I*mām al-Ghazālī, in this quotation, explains how new
knowledge may be derived from previously known
information. The quotation is epistemological in

29. Al-Ghazālī, *Iḥyā' ʿUlūm al-Dīn*, edited by Sulaymān Dunyā,
Beirut: Dār al-Maʿrifah, p. 425.

nature, but the implication for spirituality is clear. Ratiocination is the result of combining at least two previously known pieces of information in order to bring forth a third one based on what is known.

There is a big difference between believing someone on the basis of one statement, and working out new knowledge based on at least two premises. In the first instance, it is nothing but imitation, reproducing the same content, and according to al-Ghazālī, this cannot be called 'knowledge'. There is no new knowledge generated except that there is one more believer.

Al-Ghazālī had a serious problem with this state of mind. In *Deliverance from Error*, he refers to the state of natural disposition (*fiṭrah*), which is synonymous in the Islamic worldview with pure monotheism or *tawḥīd*. This state is typically corrupted by Jewish, Christian and Magian (i.e., followers of Zoroastrianism) parents. For who else is responsible for the differences among children, when they were born into an egalitarian state of natural disposition? This diversion can later on be enhanced by the clergy or teachers. The same logic applies to Muslim parents who might diverge from the Islamic worldview because of existing cultural norms that override Islam *per se*.

Other than methodology, the example that Imām al-Ghazālī uses is about the question as to which state of eternal life preferable to live of the Hereafter. For those who are absorbed in this temporary life and would like to turn to the Hereafter, because it is everlasting, either they believe in it, through the report of one person or by using two premises and then reaching the same conclusion:

> That which lasts longer is preferred.
> The Hereafter lasts longer.
> Therefore, the Hereafter is preferred.

The pleasures of this life, lawful or not, are short-lived. The pleasures of the Hereafter are everlasting. The problem is that the Hereafter has another option in store: everlasting pain. The other comparison is between short-lived pain in this world, compared to a perpetual state of pain in the Hereafter.

28

Remembering Death

اِعْلَمْ أَنَّ الْمُنْهَمِكَ فِي الدُّنْيَا الْمُكِبَّ عَلَى غُرُورِهَا الْمُحِبَّ لِشَهَوَاتِهَا
يَغْفُلُ قَلْبُهُ لَا مَحَالَةَ عَنْ ذِكْرِ الْمَوْتِ فَلَا يَذْكُرُهُ. وَإِذَا
ذُكِّرَ بِهِ كَرِهَهُ وَنَفَرَ مِنْهُ أُولَئِكَ هُمُ الَّذِينَ قَالَ اللهُ فِيهِمْ:
قُلْ إِنَّ الْمَوْتَ الَّذِي تَفِرُّونَ مِنْهُ فَإِنَّهُ مُلَاقِيكُمْ ثُمَّ تُرَدُّونَ إِلَى
عَالِمِ الْغَيْبِ وَالشَّهَادَةِ فَيُنَبِّئُكُمْ بِمَا كُنْتُمْ تَعْمَلُونَ.
(سُورَةُ الْجُمُعَةِ: ٨) ثُمَّ النَّاسُ إِمَّا مُنْهَمِكٌ، وَإِمَّا تَائِبٌ مُبْتَدِئٍ،
أَوْ عَارِفٌ مُنْتَهٍ. أَمَّا الْمُنْهَمِكُ فَلَا يَذْكُرُهُ لِلتَّأَسُّفِ عَلَى
دُنْيَاهُ وَيَشْتَغِلُ بِمَذَمَّتِهِ، وَهَذَا يَزِيدُهُ ذِكْرُ الْمَوْتِ مِنَ اللهِ بُعْدًا.
وَأَمَّا التَّائِبُ: فَإِنَّهُ يُكْثِرُ مِنْ ذِكْرِ الْمَوْتِ لِيَنْبَعِثَ بِهِ مِنْ قَلْبِهِ
الْخَوْفُ وَالْخَشْيَةُ فَيَفِي بِتَمَامِ التَّوْبَةِ وَرُبَّمَا يَكْرَهُ الْمَوْتَ خِيفَةً
مِنْ أَنْ يَخْتَطِفَهُ قَبْلَ تَمَامِ التَّوْبَةِ قَبْلَ إِصْلَاحِ الزَّادِ، وَهُوَ مَعْذُورٌ
فِي كَرَاهَةِ الْمَوْتِ وَلَا يَدْخُلُ هَذَا تَحْتَ قَوْلِهِ صَلَّى اللهُ عَلَيْهِ
وَسَلَّمَ: (مَنْ كَرِهَ لِقَاءَ اللهِ كَرِهَ اللهُ لِقَاءَهُ)، فَإِنَّ هَذَا لَيْسَ يَكْرَهُ

المَوْتَ وَلِقَاءَهِ اللهِ وَإِنَّمَا يَخَافُ فَوْتَ لِقَاءِ اللهِ لِقُصُورِهِ وَتَقْصِيرِهِ،

وَهُوَ كَالَّذِي يَتَأَخَّرُ عَنْ لِقَاءِ الحَبِيبِ مُشْتَغِلاً بِالاِسْتِعْدَادِ لِلِقَائِهِ

عَلَى وَجْهٍ يَرْضَاهُ فَلا يَعُدُّ كَارِهاً لِلِقَائِهِ. وَعَلامَةُ هَذَا أَنْ يَكُونَ

دَائِمَ الاِسْتِعْدَادِ لَهُ لا شُغْلَ لَهُ سِوَاهُ وَإِلَّا الْتَحَقَ بِالمُنْهَمِكِ فِي

الدُّنْيَا، وَأَمَّا العَارِفُ: فَإِنَّهُ يَذْكُرُ المَوْتَ دَائِماً، لِأَنَّهُ مَوْعِدُ

لِقَائِهِ لِحَبِيبِهِ، وَالمُحِبُّ لا يَنْسَى قَطُّ مَوْعِدَ لِقَاءِ الحَبِيبِ.[30]

Know that if one who is preoccupied with this world, is devoted to its delusion and is in love with its lusts his heart will inevitably forget to remember death, and so he does not remember it. And if he is reminded of it, he hates it and is repelled by it. These are the ones about whom Allah said: *Say, 'Indeed, the death from which you flee – it will meet you. Then you will be returned to the Knower of the unseen and the witnessed, and He will inform you about what you used to do.'* (Qur'ān 62:8) People, in this respect, are either someone who is preoccupied [with this worldly life], someone who has repented but is still at the beginning of his journey, or an accomplished Gnostic. As for the one who is preoccupied [with this worldly life], he does not mention death out of regret for his world. He also busies himself dispraising death, which only increases his remoteness from Allah. As for the person who has repented, he mentions death often in order that dread of Allah emanates from his heart, so that he perfects his repentance. He may detest death for fear of being overtaken by it before perfecting

---

30. Al-Ghazālī, *Iḥyā' 'Ulūm al-Dīn*, edited by Sulaymān Dunyā, Beirut: Dār al-Ma'rifah, p. 449.

his repentance and before being able to secure his provisions [for the Hereafter]. [In this case] he is excused in his hatred of death. The *ḥadīth* of the Prophet ﷺ: 'He who hates meeting God, Allah hates meeting him' does not apply to him. For [in this instance,] he does not hate death or meeting Allah, rather he is worried about missing the meeting of Allah because of his shortcomings and failings. He is like someone who is late for meeting the beloved because of being busy preparing himself to meet him in a way that pleases him, so he cannot be someone who hates meeting him. As for the Gnostic, he constantly remembers death because it is the appointment for meeting the Beloved, and the lover never forgets the appointment with his beloved.

*D*eath! No matter how one chooses to react to it, it is inevitable and will bring all the joys and sorrows of this life to an end, but only of this life, for the next one is either for one's advantage or against it, where pain and pleasure mix no more. And if one runs away from death, one will find it wherever one goes, or rather it will find one wherever one goes: *Wherever you may be, death will overtake you, even if you should be within towers of lofty construction...* (Qur'ān 4:78)

This is why one of humanity's biggest concerns revolves around death, whether it marks the end or it is simply a gate into a different realm. From the *Epic of Gilgamesh* to cryonics, the idea is to become immortal here and now, but this is simply not possible. Allah created life and death to see who is willing to do what is beautiful: *[He] who created death and life to test you [as to] which of you is best in deed – and He is the Exalted in Might, the Forgiving.* (Qur'ān 67:2)

One is distracted by this life to the extent that one forgets about death, the Hereafter and Allah. And when is reminded about it, one dismisses it as if it can be postponed indefinitely, or as if there is no life after death. Distractions include commuting, working, running errands, headphones blasting music, looking for fun on weekends, binge drinking or doing drugs, overeating, watching brain-numbing TV programmes, checking social media immediately before sleeping and upon waking up, being a single parent preoccupied with childcare, depression and seeing a therapist.

One must be conscious of death, modifying one's behaviour accordingly, and be mindful of the limitations of this life and still be satisfied with one's share of this life. Remembering death does not cancel life. It positively frames it within the right perspective. The lovers of Allah love to be with Him. Death brings one closer to that encounter. Those who are conscious of His presence have a spiritual system of checks and balances that helps in guiding them in this life in preparation for the next.

29

Knowledge vs. Gold and Silver

وَاعْلَمْ أَنَّ الشَّيْءَ النَّفِيسَ المَرْغُوبَ فِيهِ يَنْقَسِمُ إِلَى مَا يُطْلَبُ
لِغَيْرِهِ وَإِلَى مَا يُطْلَبُ لِذَاتِهِ وَإِلَى مَا يُطْلَبُ لِغَيْرِهِ وَلِذَاتِهِ جَمِيعاً.
فَمَا يُطْلَبُ لِذَاتِهِ أَشْرَفُ وَأَفْضَلُ مِمَّا يُطْلَبُ لِغَيْرِهِ، وَالمَطْلُوبُ
لِغَيْرِهِ: الدَّرَاهِمُ وَالدَّنَانِيرُ فَإِنَّهُمَا حَجَرَانِ لَا مَنْفَعَةَ لَهُمَا. وَلَوْلَا
أَنَّ اللهَ سُبْحَانَهُ وَتَعَالَى يَسَّرَ قَضَاءَ الحَاجَاتِ بِهِمَا لَكَانَا
وَالحَصْبَاءُ بِمَثَابَةٍ وَاحِدَةٍ. وَالَّذِي يُطْلَبُ لِذَاتِهِ فَالسَّعَادَةُ فِي
الآخِرَةِ وَلَذَّةُ النَّظَرِ لِوَجْهِ اللهِ تَعَالَى. وَالَّذِي يُطْلَبُ لِذَاتِهِ وَلِغَيْرِهِ
فَكَسَلَامَةِ البَدَنِ، فَإِنَّ سَلَامَةَ الرَّجُلِ مَثَلاً مَطْلُوبَةٌ مِنْ حَيْثُ
إِنَّهَا سَلَامَةٌ لِلْبَدَنِ عَنِ الأَلَمِ وَمَطْلُوبَةٌ لِلْمَشْيِ بِهَا وَالتَّوَصُّلِ إِلَى
المَآرِبِ وَالحَاجَاتِ. وَهَذَا الاعْتِبَارُ إِذَا نَظَرْتَ إِلَى العِلْمِ
رَأَيْتَهُ لَذِيذاً فِي نَفْسِهِ فَيَكُونُ مَطْلُوباً بِالذَّاتِهِ، وَوَجَدْتَهُ وَسِيلَةً إِلَى

دَارِ الآخِرَةِ وَسَعَادَتِهَا وَذَرِيعَةٌ إِلَى القُرْبِ مِنَ اللهِ تَعَالَى

وَلَا يُتَوَصَّلُ إِلَيْهَا إِلَّا بِالعِلْمِ وَالعَمَلِ وَلَا يُتَوَصَّلُ إِلَى العَمَلِ

إِلَّا بِالعِلْمِ بِكَيْفِيَّةِ العَمَلِ. فَأَصْلُ السَّعَادَةِ فِي الدُّنْيَا وَالآخِرَةِ هُوَ

العِلْمُ. فَهُوَ إِذَنْ أَفْضَلُ الأَعْمَالِ، وَكَيْفَ لَا وَقَدْ تُعْرَفُ فَضِيلَةُ

الشَّيْءِ أَيْضاً بِشَرَفِ ثَمَرَتِهِ؟ وَقَدْ عَرَفْتَ أَنَّ ثَمَرَةَ العِلْمِ القُرْبُ

مِنْ رَبِّ العَالَمِينَ وَالِالتِحَاقُ بِأُفُقِ المَلَائِكَةِ وَمُقَارَنَةُ المَلَأِ

الأَعْلَى، هَذَا فِي الآخِرَةِ وَأَمَّا فِي الدُّنْيَا فَالعِزُّ وَالوَقَارُ وَنُفُوذُ

الحُكْمِ عَلَى المُلُوكِ وَلُزُومُ الِاحْتِرَامِ فِي الطِّبَاعِ.[31]

Know that any precious, desired thing belongs to one of two categories: that which is sought for other than itself, that which sought for itself, or sought for both other than itself and itself. That which is sought for other than itself are gold and silver, for they are two stones of no benefit [in themselves], and if it were not that Allah has made them the means to facilitate the fulfilment of needs, they would be no different than pebbles. As for that which is sought for itself, it is felicity in the Hereafter and the pleasure of having a beatific vision of the face of Allah Most High. That which is sought for itself and other than itself is like the wellbeing of the body. The fitness of the leg, for example, is sought because it is a necessary part of the wellbeing of the body and because it is required for walking and reaching ends and needs. Accordingly, if you look at knowledge, you will find it pleasurable in itself, which makes it therefore sought

31. Al-Ghazālī, *Iḥyā' 'Ulūm al-Dīn*, edited by Sulaymān Dunyā, Beirut: Dār al-Maʿrifah, p. 12.

for itself. You will also find it a means to felicity in the Hereafter and to the pleasure of the beatific vision of Allah Most High. This is only achieved through knowledge and action, and action can only be achieved through the knowledge of how to act. It follows that the root of felicity in this world and the Hereafter is knowledge. Therefore, seeking knowledge is the best of deeds. How could it not be, when the merit of something is also known through the honourable character of its fruit? And you have already known that the fruit of knowledge is proximity to Allah and joining the status of the angels and being compared to the Highest Plenum [of the angels]. This is in the Hereafter. As for this world, it is dignity and esteem, issuing edicts that even kings cannot escape, and commanding respect naturally.

*I*t is strange that gold and silver are never shiny enough to blind people! Imām al-Ghazālī is right; if it were not for the fact that Allah guided people to their use, gold and silver would be as precious as gravel.

Things are either sought for something else or for themselves. Money is sought for the essentials of life: food, medicine, clothing and shelter. Money should not be sought for itself, for that would be against the right relationship that one should have with it. It is legitimate to save money for genuine reasons such as education or retirement. The Prophet ﷺ made it clear that the best money is the money spent on one's family. Hoarding money, on the other hand, is an unacceptable behaviour: *...And those who* *hoard gold and silver and spend it not in the way of Allah – give them tidings of a painful punishment.* (Qur'ān 9:34) Hoarding money is practically nothing but removing it from circulation, which is the life of the economy. Hoarding has therefore a negative impact on the community.

That which is sought for its own intrinsic value includes happiness in the Hereafter, and the beatific vision, which is the unmediated vision of Allah in Heaven. Happiness here should not be conflated with the problematic concepts associated with material wealth, fame, and status. All of these will wither away, unless they are for the sake of Allah, which is very hard to see in reality. Happy is the one who makes it to Heaven.

As for what is sought for both its inherent value and also because it is a vehicle for something else, this cannot apply except to knowledge. Knowledge is enjoyable. This is why true scholars immerse themselves in a contemplative state of mind and heart, examining text and reality, and expressing their thoughts in writing, all in seclusion. They do not miss much outside their niche of education, except for that which is imperative to attend to. Yet, knowledge is also sought for its fruit; which is bringing the servant closer to Allah. Knowledge is a prerequisite for action which is considered a condition for happiness in this world and the Hereafter.

30

Presenting Faith
to Children

اِعْلَمْ أَنَّ مَا ذَكَرْنَاهُ فِي تَرْجَمَةِ الْعَقِيدَةِ يَنْبَغِي أَنْ يُقَدَّمَ إِلَى
الصَّبِيِّ فِي أَوَّلِ نُشُوءِهِ لِيَحْفَظَهُ حِفْظًا ثُمَّ لَا يَزَالُ يَنْكَشِفُ لَهُ مَعْنَاهُ
فِي كِبَرِهِ شَيْئًا فَشَيْئًا؛ فَابْتِدَاؤُهُ الْحِفْظُ ثُمَّ الْفَهْمُ ثُمَّ الِاعْتِقَادُ
وَالْإِيقَانُ وَالتَّصْدِيقُ بِهِ، وَذَلِكَ مِمَّا يَحْصُلُ فِي الصَّبِيِّ بِغَيْرِ
بُرْهَانٍ. فَمِنْ فَضْلِ اللهِ سُبْحَانَهُ عَلَى قَلْبِ الْإِنْسَانِ أَنْ شَرَحَهُ
فِي أَوَّلِ نُشُوءِهِ لِلْإِيمَانِ مِنْ غَيْرِ حَاجَةٍ إِلَى حُجَّةٍ أَوْ بُرْهَانٍ، وَكَيْفَ
يُنْكَرُ ذَلِكَ وَجَمِيعُ عَقَائِدِ الْعَوَامِّ مَبَادِيهَا التَّلْقِينُ الْمُجَرَّدُ وَالتَّقْلِيدُ
الْمَحْضُ؟ نَعَمْ يَكُونُ الِاعْتِقَادُ الْحَاصِلُ بِمُجَرَّدِ التَّقْلِيدِ غَيْرَ خَالٍ
عَنْ نَوْعٍ مِنَ الضَّعْفِ فِي الِابْتِدَاءِ عَلَى مَعْنَى أَنَّهُ يَقْبَلُ الْإِزَالَةَ

بِنَقِيضِهِ لَوْ أُلْقِيَ إِلَيْهِ فَلَابُدَّ مِنْ تَقْوِيَتِهِ وَإِثْبَاتِهِ فِي نَفْسِ العَامِّي
حَتَّى يَتَرَسَّخَ وَلَا يَتَزَلْزَلَ. [32]

Know that what we have mentioned when explaining
the tenets of faith should be introduced to the child at
the beginning of their growth, so that they memorises
it. Its meaning will then keep unfolding to them little by
little as they get older. So, its beginning is memorisation,
then understanding, and then belief, certitude and assent,
which occurs in the child without proof. It is the favour of
Allah Almighty bestowed upon the human heart that He
expanded it for faith at the beginning of his growth without any need for proof or demonstration. And how can
this be denied when the bases of the tenets of faith of the
masses are based on pure instruction and imitation? Yes,
belief resulting from pure imitation is not initially devoid
of a kind of weakness, in the sense that it is likely to be
replaced with its opposite if presented to him. Therefore,
it must be strengthened and affirmed in the child and the
uneducated so that it is firmly-rooted and unshakeable.

Al-Ghazālī had an amazing understanding of human
psychology and education, especially concerning
teaching children. He proposed to begin with children
memorising the tenets of faith. Understanding, he
explains, takes place gradually over a long period
of time. It is then, after understanding, that belief

32. Al-Ghazālī, *Iḥyā' ʿUlūm al-Dīn*, edited by Sulaymān Dunyā,
Beirut: Dār al-Maʿrifah, p. 94.

takes place, to be followed by certitude and assent. Children need no proof and this is a gift from Allah.

The minds of children should be given utmost care. They should be nurtured and educated. Imām al-Ghazālī wanted children to have a solid faith which is not based on imitation. Imitation may be problematic because it reflects a state which is widespread among the common people, for whom imitation may allow alternative worldviews to replace each other. Imitation is a weak state which needs to be strengthened and affirmed, so that it cannot be shaken. Al-Ghazālī is calling here for the protection of the faith of the average person who is dependent on imitation.

This quotation provides an opportunity to question what formal and informal education is given to children today, without ruining their childhood but also without missing out on universal Islamic social values and ethics. The answer will vary today according to national educational policies, cultural influences and future, professional expectations. The educational system propagated in the traditional madrasa, though it plays an important role in teaching religious subjects, is reductionist at best, and usually does not provide enough sciences and maths or social sciences. Imām al-Ghazālī is of the opinion that a community is literally sinning if it cannot produce much needed professionals.

There is no doubt that faith is essential for this life and the Hereafter, and education should deal with this issue. But it should never be a matter of choosing between studying theology or the exact sciences. The true Islamic worldview considers both fields of knowledge as integral components. One of them is based on studying the Revealed Book (i.e., the Qur'ān) and the other studies the revealed book of nature, the universe, for both of them come from Allah. In Arabic, verses of the Qur'ān and marvellous natural phenomena are designated by the same term: *āyāt* (plural of *āyah*).

External Cleansing and Internal Purification

والطَّهَارَةُ لَهَا أَرْبَعُ مَرَاتِبَ (الْمَرْتَبَةُ الأُولَى) تَطْهِيرُ الظَّاهِرِ عَنِ
الأَحْدَاثِ وَعَنِ الأَخْبَاثِ وَالفَضَلاَتِ، (الْمَرْتَبَةُ الثَّانِيَةُ)
تَطْهِيرُ الجَوَارِحِ عَنِ الجَرَائِمِ وَالآثَامِ، (الْمَرْتَبَةُ الثَّالِثَةُ)
تَطْهِيرُ القَلْبِ عَنِ الأَخْلاَقِ المَذْمُومَةِ وَالرَّذَائِلِ المَمْقُوتَةِ،
(الْمَرْتَبَةُ الرَّابِعَةُ) تَطْهِيرُ السِّرِّ عَمَّا سِوَى اللهِ تَعَالَى وَهِيَ
طَهَارَةُ الأَنْبِيَاءِ صَلَوَاتُ اللهِ عَلَيْهِمْ وَالصِّدِّيقِينَ. [33]

And purification has four levels: The first is the
purification of the outward from physical impurities,
dirt and filth; the second is the purification of the limbs
from crimes and sins; the third is the purification of
the heart from all blameworthy traits and abominable
vices; the fourth is the purification of the inmost secret

---

33. Al-Ghazālī, *Iḥyā' ʿUlūm al-Dīn*, edited by Sulaymān Dunyā,
Beirut: Dār al-Maʿrifah, p. 126.

from everything other than Allah Most High, which is the purification of the Prophets ﷺ and the veracious among the righteous.

*C*leanliness and purification, both physical and spiritual, are healthy signs in any person. The first level of purification has excellent implications for hygiene, but this would be an oversimplification of what the purification of the outward means. Getting rid of tangible impurities is a must, to the best of one's knowledge and as much as circumstances permit it, and that is still the first step. Imām al-Ghazālī wanted people who perform ablution to think about the water running down their faces and limbs as if their sins were taken away with it.

It is in this light that one may understand the following part of a *ḥadīth* in which the Prophet ﷺ said: 'Purification is half of faith...' (Narrated by Muslim). In another *ḥadīth*, the Prophet ﷺ speaks about the effect of the five daily prayers and gives the simile of a person who cleans himself by a river five times a day. Just as the water of this river will clean him of all his dirt, the prayers, too, will cleanse him of all his sins.

The second level of purification is achieved by protecting the outward limbs and organs from engaging in criminal and sinful acts: washing the mouth of the residues of cursing, backbiting, false witness and lying, to name but a few ills, which the tongue is capable of; washing the eyes of what they are deliberately, not accidently, exposed to; washing the hands of the impurities of stealing and violence; and washing the feet of the dirt accumulated from walking deliberately on wrong paths, in the wrong directions, for the wrong reasons.

The third level of purification is purely spiritual. It is time to turn to the heart and purify it from all that is negative and sinful. The heart should not harbour ill feelings or wrong intentions, nor embark on any activity that is on a collision course with Revelation or the Prophetic path. The heart is now ready for the last phase, the purification of the prophets, which is making it an exclusive dwelling for the recollection of the name of Allah.

32

Deconstructing
Distractions

اِعْلَمْ أَنَّ الْمُؤْمِنَ لَابُدَّ أَنْ يَكُونَ مُعَظِّماً لَلهِ عَزَّ وَجَلَّ وَخَائِفاً مِنْهُ
وَرَاجِياً لَهُ وَمُسْتَجِيراً مِنْ تَقْصِيرِهِ فَلَا يَنْفَكُّ عَنْ هَذِهِ الْأَحْوَالِ
بَعْدَ إِيمَانِهِ، وَإِنْ كَانَتْ قُوَّتُهَا بِقَدْرِ قُوَّةِ يَقِينِهِ فَانْفِكَاكُهُ عَنْهَا فِي
الصَّلَاةِ لَا سَبَبَ لَهُ إِلَّا تَفَرُّقُ الفِكْرِ وَتَقْسِيمُ الخَاطِرِ وَغَيْبَةُ
القَلْبِ عَنِ المُنَاجَاةِ وَالغَفْلَةِ عَنِ الصَّلَاةِ. وَلَا يُلْهِي عَنِ الصَّلَاةِ
إِلَّا الخَوَاطِرُ الوَارِدَةُ الشَّاغِلَةُ. فَالدَّوَاءُ فِي إِحْضَارِ القَلْبِ هُوَ
دَفْعُ تِلْكَ الخَوَاطِرِ وَلَا يُدْفَعُ الشَّيْءُ إِلَّا بِدَفْعِ سَبَبِهِ
فَلْتَعْلَمْ سَبَبَهُ. وَسَبَبُ مَوَارِدِ الخَوَاطِرِ إِمَّا أَنْ يَكُونَ أَمْراً
خَارِجاً أَوْ أَمْراً فِي ذَاتِهِ بَاطِناً.[34]

---

34. Al-Ghazālī, *Iḥyāʾ ʿUlūm al-Dīn*, edited by Sulaymān Dunyā,
Beirut: Dār al-Maʿrifah, p. 163.

Know that the believer must glorify Allah, glorified and exalted is He, fear Him, have hope in Him and seek refuge [in Him] due to his shortcomings. He should not be without these states after having faith. And even though the strength of these states is commensurate with the strength of his certitude, being without them during the prayer has no reason except the dissipation of his thoughts, his divided mind, the absence of his heart from entreating [Allah] and heedlessness in the prayer. Nothing distracts from the prayer except incoming thoughts which busy one. The cure for this is to have a presence of heart, i.e. driving away these incoming thoughts. However, a thing can be driven away only by driving away its cause. Therefore, know its cause and the cause of these incoming thoughts may be external or something essentially internal.

To be distracted, or not to be distracted, this is the essence of the problem. We allow the slings and arrows of materialism and lowly issues to be aimed at us and we deprive ourselves of being conscious in the presence of Allah. This is not the optimal state of a heart that was created to know Him.

The believer glorifies Allah, alternates between fear and hope and seeks refuge in Him from his own shortcomings. And if and when the heart is split between numerous attractions, it becomes lacking in intimate talk with Allah. But while in the prayer, the body should be facing towards Makkah while the heart is with Allah.

The sources of distraction, which prevent concentration, are either external or internal. And the solution to these distractions lies in uprooting their causes.

External distraction may be visual, auditory or due to uncomfortable physical conditions. One may find these solutions in the Sunnah of the Prophet ﷺ. Regarding visual distractions, Muslims are advised, while praying, to look at the spot where they put their foreheads upon prostration. This way, they will be able to minimise the possibility of visual distraction. When it comes to auditory distractions, one cannot raise one's voice in the mosque even when reciting the Holy Qur'ān or upon supplications. Today, we experience problems associated with the sound systems in mosques, such as in microphones or loudspeakers. One needs to turn to professionals when dealing with technical issues. Cell phones ringing various tones while in the prayer should definitely not be tolerated. Putting the cell phone on silent mode might be helpful to others, but once one receives a call, it vibrates, and that is also a source of distraction. Other physical distractions include the quality of air. Muslims are prohibited from going to the mosque for congregational prayer after eating onion or garlic because their smell is offensive.

The internal sources of distractions are mainly thoughts and feelings. All that is negative should be constantly pushed away. Positive ideas and feel-ings which are not related to the prayer, such as planning to help the needy people, can wait until after the prayer.

33

Fasting Has Three Degrees

اِعْلَمْ أَنَّ الصَّوْمَ ثَلَاثُ دَرَجَاتٍ: صَوْمُ الْعُمُومِ وَصَوْمُ الْخُصُوصِ
وَصَوْمُ خُصُوصِ الْخُصُوصِ. أَمَّا صَوْمُ الْعُمُومِ فَهُوَ كَفُّ الْبَطْنِ
وَالْفَرْجِ عَنْ قَضَاءِ الشَّهْوَةِ كَمَا سَبَقَ تَفْصِيلُهُ. وَأَمَّا صَوْمُ الْخُصُوصِ
فَهُوَ كَفُّ السَّمْعِ وَالْبَصَرِ وَاللِّسَانِ وَالْيَدِ وَالرِّجْلِ وَسَائِرِ الْجَوَارِحِ
عَنِ الآثَامِ. وَأَمَّا صَوْمُ خُصُوصِ الْخُصُوصِ فَصَوْمُ الْقَلْبِ عَنِ
الْهِمَمِ الدَّنِيَّةِ وَالأَفْكَارِ الدُّنْيَوِيَّةِ وَكَفُّهُ عَمَّا سِوَى اللهِ عَزَّ وَجَلَّ
بِالْكُلِّيَّةِ، وَيَحْصُلُ الْفِطْرُ فِي هَذَا الصَّوْمِ بِالْفِكْرِ فِيمَا سِوَى اللهِ
عَزَّ وَجَلَّ وَالْيَوْمِ الآخِرِ وَبِالْفِكْرِ فِي الدُّنْيَا إِلَّا دُنْيَا تُرَادُ لِلتَّدَيُّنِ،
فَإِنَّ ذَلِكَ مِنْ زَادِ الآخِرَةِ وَلَيْسَ مِنَ الدُّنْيَا.[35]

---

35. Al-Ghazālī, *Iḥyāʾ ʿUlūm al-Dīn*, edited by Sulaymān Dunyā, Beirut: Dār al-Maʿrifah, p. 234.

Know that fasting has three degrees: the fasting of common people, the fasting of the elite amongst people, and the fasting of the elect among the elite. As for the fasting of common people, it is preventing the belly and the private parts from fulfilling their desire, as it was explained in detail before. The fasting of the elite is preventing the hearing, sight, tongue, hands, legs and all other limbs from committing sins. The fasting of the elect among the elite is the abstinence of the heart from lowly aspirations and worldly thoughts, and completely restraining it from other than Allah, glorified and exalted is He. Breaking the fast in this kind of fasting takes place by thinking about other than Allah Most High or the Day of Judgment, unless this thinking about this world is intended for the sake of the religion, in which case it is considered part of the provisions of the Hereafter and not this world.

*I*mām al-Ghazālī's revivalist paradigm in *Revival of the Religious Sciences* is about bringing to life the most important dimension in all forms of worship: spirituality.

He was critical of the jurists who produced detailed accounts of what the prayer, fasting and the Pilgrimage are, among a host of other acts of worship, and forgot about the role of the heart in all this.

Fasting in classical works of jurisprudence (i.e., *fiqh*) is defined as abstinence from eating, drinking and having sexual relations between husband and wife, from dawn to sunset, during the lunar month of Ramadan. It has been noticed, year after year, that the questions of the Muslim community during Ramadan are usually about actions that nullify fasting or how to compensate for missed days because of sickness or travel, etc. Questions about how to benefit spiritually from Ramadan, or the role of the heart in fasting, are a rarity.

There are methods of dieting today that require fasting for as long as sixteen hours a day. The intention here is losing weight, not spirituality. As long as one does not intend to fast for the sake of Allah, then fasting is in vain. The same applies when one explains the five daily prayers in terms of physical exercise, and the Pilgrimage in terms of tourism, for in such a case the act of worship becomes null and void. Rather than bringing one closer to Allah, it makes one more distant from Him.

The same thing also applies to the higher level of abstinence, that of the limbs. For what good is it if one stops eating and drinking lawful things while allowing one's eyes the freedom to visually consume what is prohibited? What benefit does one draw from not eating or drinking while one's tongue and ears indulge in backbiting? All the limbs, with no exception, should participate in abstinence throughout one's life and not just during Ramadan.

The highest level of abstinence is that of the heart. The heart should abstain from everything other than Allah. Recollecting His beautiful names and attributes requires clearing the heart of worldly attachments. Those who are capable of doing this are the friends of Allah.

34

Liberation from Attachments

وَأَمَّا قَطْعُ العَلَائِقِ فَمَعْنَاهُ رَدُّ المَظَالِمِ وَالتَّوْبَةُ الخَالِصَةُ لِلَّهِ تَعَالَى عَنْ جُمْلَةِ المَعَاصِي. فَكُلُّ مَظْلَمَةٍ عَلَاقَةٌ وَكُلُّ عَلَاقَةٍ مِثْلُ غَرِيمٍ حَاضِرٍ مُتَعَلِّقٍ بِتَلَابِيبِهِ يُنَادِي عَلَيْهِ وَيَقُولُ: إِلَى أَيْنَ تَتَوَجَّهُ؟ أَتَقْصِدُ بَيْتَ مَلِكِ المُلُوكِ وَأَنْتَ مُضَيِّعٌ أَمْرَهُ فِي مَنْزِلِكَ هَذَا وَمُسْتَهِينٌ بِهِ وَمُهْمِلٌ لَهُ؟ أَوَلَا تَسْتَحِي أَنْ تَقْدَمَ عَلَيْهِ قُدُومَ العَبْدِ العَاصِي فَيَرُدَّكَ وَلَا يَقْبَلُكَ؟ فَإِنْ كُنْتَ رَاغِباً فِي قَبُولِ زِيَارَتِكَ فَنَفِّذْ أَوَامِرَهُ وَرُدَّ المَظَالِمَ وَتُبْ إِلَيْهِ أَوَّلاً مِنْ جَمِيعِ المَعَاصِي وَاقْطَعْ عَلَاقَةَ قَلْبِكَ عَنِ الِالْتِفَاتِ إِلَى مَا وَرَاءَكَ لِتَكُونَ مُتَوَجِّهاً إِلَيْهِ بِوَجْهِ قَلْبِكَ كَمَا أَنَّكَ مُتَوَجِّهٌ إِلَى بَيْتِهِ بِوَجْهٍ ظَاهِرِكَ. فَإِنْ لَمْ تَفْعَلْ ذَلِكَ لَمْ يَكُنْ لَكَ مِنْ سَفَرِكَ أَوَّلاً إِلَّا النَّصَبُ وَالشَّقَاءُ وَآخِراً إِلَّا الطَّرْدُ وَالرَّدُّ. وَلْيَقْطَعِ العَلَائِقَ عَنْ وَطَنِهِ انْقِطَاعَ مَنْ

قُطِعَ عَنْهُ وَقُدِّرَ أَنْ لا يَعُودَ إِلَيْهِ وَلْيَكْتُبْ وَصِيَّتَهُ لِأَوْلادِهِ وَأَهْلِهِ

فَإِنَّ الْمُسَافِرَ وَمَالَهُ لَعَلَى خَطَرٍ إِلّا مَنْ وَقَى اللهُ سُبْحَانَهُ.

وَلْيَتَذَكَّرْ عِنْدَ قَطْعِهِ الْعَلائِقَ لِسَفَرِ الْحَجِّ قَطْعَ الْعَلائِقِ لِسَفَرِ

الآخِرَةِ فَإِنَّ ذَلِكَ بَيْنَ يَدَيْهِ عَلَى الْقُرْبِ وَمَا يُقَدِّمُهُ مِنْ هَذَا السَّفَرِ

طَمَعٌ فِي تَيْسِيرِ ذَلِكَ السَّفَرِ فَهُوَ الْمُسْتَقَرُّ وَإِلَيْهِ الْمَصِيرُ فَلا يَنْبَغِي

أَنْ يَغْفَلَ عَنْ ذَلِكَ السَّفَرِ عَنِ الاسْتِعْدَادِ بِهَذَا السَّفَرِ. ٣٦

As for cutting off attachments, it means making amends
to those one has wronged and repentance to Allah Most
High from all sins. For every iniquity is an attachment
and every attachment is like an antagonist who is seizing
one by the collar, shouting at him: 'Where are you going?
Are you heading for the house of the King of kings while
neglecting His command in this dwelling of yours, which
you have discarded and ignored? Are you not ashamed
of yourself going to Him as a disobedient servant, not
fearing that He will send you back and not accept you?
If you wish your visit to be accepted, then you should
fulfil His commands, make reparations regarding all
iniquities, repent to Him from all the sins and cut off
your heart's attachment by not looking back to what
is behind you, so that you will be directing the face of
your heart towards Him, just as you turn your outward
face towards His house. If you do not do this, then
you will first gain from this travel nothing but toil and
wretchedness and, at the end, nothing but expulsion

---

36. Al-Ghazālī, *Iḥyāʾ ʿUlūm al-Dīn*, edited by Sulaymān Dunyā,
Beirut: Dār al-Maʿrifah, p. 267.

and rejection.' Let the traveller sever his attachment with his home country exactly like a stranded traveller who is destined never to return. He should write his final will for his children and family, for the traveller and his money are in danger except the one whom Allah, glorified is He, protects. He should remember, when cutting off his attachments in preparation for the *Ḥajj* journey, to cut off his attachments when preparing for the journey to the Hereafter, for it is right before him, at a close distance. Whatever he spends in *this* journey is done in anticipation of facilitating *that* journey as it is the ultimate destination and final return. It is not fitting to be distracted by *this* journey from preparing oneself for *that* journey.

People often forget about their true origins. They often mention nation-states or geographical regions. The real story though is that humanity began in the Garden, and then expulsion from it happened because of Adam and Eve's fall (The Qur'ān has an egalitarian narrative that does not single out either one of them as eating from the Forbidden Tree first). The history of Revelation is linear, with the prophets and messengers conveying the Divine messages to humanity and the ultimate goal is to save humanity and go to Heaven.

Death takes place at an inevitable moment, which may happen to the young and the old, the healthy and the sick, the rich and the poor. But how should one prepare for death? The answer is detachment from worldly affairs. These include the unusual images of injustices clinging to anyone who has committed them, shaming him for intending to be in the presence of the King without appropriate preparation: repentance from all sins and reparations where recompense is still possible. Those who fail to live their life in a decent m anner in this world, might not be admitted into the palace of the Hereafter. Imām al-Ghazālī compares this trip to the Pilgrimage. One cannot have his body travelling in one direction while the heart is somewhere else. It is almost an existential oxymoron.

Life is a sojourn, a temporary detour, but it is definitely short. The Prophet ﷺ one day slept on a harsh mat made from leaves, and when he woke up, the impressions of the mat were visible on him. The Companions suggested getting for the Prophet ﷺ a comfortable mattress. But he responded by saying: 'What do I have to do with [the material luxuries of] your world? I am in this world but a traveller who has stopped to rest under a tree and then goes on and leaves the tree [behind].'

In this life, people behave as those in transit at airports, few have access to 'VIP' clubs and lounges, most hang around public areas. Ultimately, they all have to leave behind whatever level of comfort they had there. It has nothing to do with their final destination which has two exits; only one of them leads to eternal bliss.

35

Involvement of the Tongue, Intellect and Heart in Reciting the Holy Qur'an

وَتِلاوَةُ القُرآنِ حَقَّ تِلاوَتِهِ هُوَ أَنْ يَشْتَرِكَ فِيهِ اللِّسَانُ والعَقْلُ
والقَلبُ، فَحَظُّ اللِّسَانِ تَصْحِيحُ الـحُرُوفِ بِالتَّرتِيلِ وَحَظُّ
العَقلِ تَفْسِيرُ المَعَانِي وَحَظُّ القَلْبِ الاتِّعَاظُ والتَّأَثُّرُ بِالانْزِجَارِ
وَالائْتِمَارِ. فَاللِّسَانُ يُرَتِّلُ والعَقْلُ يُتَرَجِمُ والقَلْبُ يَتَّعِظُ.³⁷

And the recitation of the Qur'ān as it ought to be
recited is when the tongue, the intellect and the heart all
participate in it. The share of the tongue is to correctly
utter the letters through applying the rules of recitation,

---

37. Al-Ghazālī, *Iḥyā' ʿUlūm al-Dīn*, edited by Sulaymān Dunyā,
Beirut: Dār al-Maʿrifah, p. 287.

and the share of the intellect is to explain the meanings,
and the share of the heart is to be admonished, feel
moved, heed the commands and desist from the prohibi-
tions. The tongue recites, the intellect interprets and
the heart gains admonition.

*T*he Holy Qur'ān, the final revealed message to mankind, is part of a long history of revelations, including the original Torah which was revealed to Moses,
the Psalms (*Zabūr*) which was revealed to David,
and the Gospel (*Injīl*) which was revealed to Jesus
Christ, peace be upon them all.

The Holy Qur'ān is a message for all humanity,
and not just for the Muslims. And it is important to
know how to read it. It was *revealed*, not inspired,
in Arabic. All translations are interpretations
that approximate the original Arabic. This is why
Muslim worshippers from all corners of the world
recite the same Qur'ān in Arabic. Reciting it, within
or outside the formal prayers, is still considered an
act of devotion.

All the readers of the Holy Qur'ān are invited to
ponder upon its meanings. This is the final message
of Allah to humanity, and one should begin with
curiosity, very much like reading the book of nature,
which comes also from the same Divine source.

The Holy Qur'ān is a book of guidance to sound
theology, ethics, morality and spirituality. The legal

content, which is very important, is but a fraction of the whole book.

Dealing with the Holy Qur'ān involves the tongue, the intellect and the heart. The tongue recites and utters the sounds according to precise rules which have been conveyed generation after generation, since the time of the Prophet ﷺ. The tongue which recites the Holy Qur'ān and recollects the name of Allah should only be used to say good things. Those who can recite the Holy Qur'ān from memory, especially, should refine their behaviour.

The intellect should be engaged with the Holy Qur'ān for meaning. While using a translation of the meaning of the Holy Qur'ān is helpful in understanding the essence of the message, a better comprehension is only possible for those who know Arabic and deal with the Arabic text. The Holy Qur'ān is one of two textual sources of the Islamic worldview, along with the compendia of sound Prophetic traditions that contain the Sunnah. The heart is the target of the message. Once the heart heeds and implements the Qur'ānic message, only good things are expected to happen, in this life and the Hereafter.

36

Knowing Allah Is a Matter of the Heart

فَشَرَفُ الإِنْسَانِ وَفَضِيلَتُهُ الَّتِي فَاقَ بِهَا جُمْلَةً مِنْ أَصْنَافِ الخَلْقِ
بِاسْتِعْدَادِهِ لِمَعْرِفَةِ اللهِ سُبْحَانَهُ، الَّتِي هِيَ فِي الدُّنْيَا جَمَالُهُ وَكَمَالُهُ
وَفَخْرُهُ، وَفِي الآخِرَةِ عُدَّتُهُ وَذُخْرُهُ، وَإِنَّمَا اسْتَعَدَّ لِلْمَعْرِفَةِ بِقَلْبِهِ
لَا بِجَارِحَةٍ مِنْ جَوَارِحِهِ. فَالقَلْبُ هُوَ العَالِمُ بِاللهِ. وَهُوَ المُتَقَرِّبُ
إِلَى اللهِ، وَهُوَ العَامِلُ لله، وَهُوَ السَّاعِي إِلَى اللهِ، وَهُوَ المُكَاشَفُ
بِمَا عِنْدَ اللهِ وَلَدَيْهِ، وَإِنَّمَا الجَوَارِحُ أَتْبَاعٌ وَخَدَمٌ وَآلَاتٌ، يَسْتَخْدِمُهَا
القَلْبُ وَيَسْتَعْمِلُهَا اسْتِعْمَالَ المَالِكِ لِلْعَبْدِ واسْتِخْدَامَ الرَّاعِي
لِلرَّعِيَّةِ والصَّانِعِ لِلآلَةِ؛ فَالقَلْبُ هُوَ المَقْبُولُ عِنْدَ اللهِ إِذَا سَلِمَ مِنْ
غَيْرِ اللهِ، وَهُوَ المَحْجُوبُ عَنِ اللهِ إِذَا صَارَ مُسْتَغْرِقاً بِغَيْرِ اللهِ،
وَهُوَ المُطَالَبُ وَهُوَ المُخَاطَبُ وَهُوَ المُعَاتَبُ وَهُوَ الَّذِي يَسْعَدُ
بِالقُرْبِ مِنَ اللهِ فَيُفْلِحُ إِذَا زَكَّاهُ، وَهُوَ الَّذِي يَخِيبُ وَيَشْقَى إِذَا

دَنَّسَهُ وَدَسَّاهُ؛ وَهُوَ الْمُطِيعُ بِالْحَقِيقَةِ لِلَّهِ تَعَالَى، وَإِنَّمَا الَّذِي يَنْتَشِرُ
عَلَى الْجَوَارِحِ مِنَ الْعِبَادَاتِ أَنْوَارُهُ، وَهُوَ الْعَاصِي الْمُتَمَرِّدُ عَلَى
اللَّهِ تَعَالَى وَإِنَّمَا السَّارِي إِلَى الْأَعْضَاءِ مِنَ الْفَوَاحِشِ آثَارُهُ؛
وَبِاظْلَامِهِ وَاسْتِنَارَتِهِ تَظْهَرُ مَحَاسِنُ الظَّاهِرِ وَمَسَاوِيهِ.[38]

The human being's honour and merit, thanks to which he
surpasses the totality of other created beings, is due to his
innate potential to know Allah Most High which is, in
this world, his beauty, perfection and pride and will be,
in the Hereafter, his asset and provision. But his aptitude
for gnosis is through his heart, not through any external
limb. For it is his heart that has knowledge of Allah,
draws near to Allah, exerts effort for the sake of Allah
and hastens to Allah just as it is the one it is to the heart
that it is revealed what Allah has in store. The limbs are
but followers, servants and tools which the heart uses
like a master uses his slave or a person of responsibility
uses those under his care or a craftsman uses his craft.

The heart is the one accepted by Allah when it is not
sullied by [attachment to] anything but Him; and it is the
one veiled from Allah when it becomes preoccupied with
other than Allah; and it is the one demanded to comply,
the one addressed and the one reprimanded; just as it is
the one that will become happy for being near Allah and
gain success if one cleanses it or will become destined
for eternal misery if one tarnishes and corrupts it. It is
in reality the heart that is obedient to Allah Most High
[rather than the mind or the limbs], for what spreads
over the limbs in the acts of worship are its lights.
And it is the heart that disobeys and rebels against

---

38. Al-Ghazālī, *Iḥyā' ʿUlūm al-Dīn*, edited by Sulaymān Dunyā,
Beirut: Dār al-Maʿrifah, vol. 4, p. 2.

Allah Most High, for the vices that manifest through
the limbs are only its signs and traces, just as it is
through its being dark or illumined that the bad
and good traits appear on the outward.

*I*t is all about knowing Allah! The heart is the vehicle
for such knowledge which forms the essence of
spiritual life. Once the heart submits to the Will
of Allah, the soul ascends and forever continues to
climb from one spiritual station to another. It will
attempt to be perpetually conscious of its Creator,
love Him and seek His mercy. At the same time, this
loving relationship, state of felicity and knowledge
of Allah have a great positive impact on other fellow
human beings and the environment through sharing
this gifted love and mercy with others and trying to
bring them to the same state of happiness.

But if the heart rebels and turns away from its
Creator, it descends into an abyss of darkness and
becomes oblivious to the light that fills the universe,
including the innumerable hearts of His true lovers.
This spiritual darkness makes it difficult for the heart
to discern between right and wrong.

It is the heart that is moved by the Divine light for
more intimate knowledge of Allah through prayer,
supplication, and contemplation. One reaches this
level when one tastes the sweetness of the relationship. A sign of those who reach this level of intimacy

is that they find refuge, comfort and spiritual nourishment in their acts of devotion. Their limbs reflect and translate the light coming from the heart into actions in line with the Divine Will.

The spiritual heart is the best gift that can be bestowed on us. Yet, there is a level of honour that has been granted to all human beings, when compared to other creatures. It is granted regardless of belief, the most important criterion in the sight of Allah: *And We have certainly honored the children of Adam and carried them on the land and sea and provided for them of the good things and preferred them over much of what We have created, with [definite] preference.* (Qur'ān 17:70)

Every human being is guaranteed protection of life, property, progeny, intellect and freedom of worship, especially for Jews and Christians who are described as People of the Book, a phrase that never fails to make them feel less far away from the Muslims.

37

Inculcating Beautiful Personal Traits

فَإِذَنْ عَرَفْتَ بِهَذَا قَطْعاً أَنَّ الأَخْلاقَ الجَمِيلَةَ يُمْكِنُ اكْتِسَابُهَا
بِالرِّيَاضَةِ وَهِيَ تَكَلُّفُ الأَفْعَالِ الصَّادِرَةِ عَنْهَا ابْتِدَاءً لِتَصِيرَ
طَبْعاً انْتِهَاءً، وَهَذَا مِنْ عَجِيبِ العَلاقَةِ بَيْنَ القَلْبِ وَالجَوَارِحِ
- أَعْنِي النَّفْسَ وَالبَدَنَ - فَإِنَّ كُلَّ صِفَةٍ تَظْهَرُ فِي القَلْبِ يَفِيضُ أَثَرُهَا
عَلَى الجَوَارِحِ حَتَّى لا تَتَحَرَّكَ إِلَّا عَلَى وِفْقِهَا لا مَحَالَةَ، وَكُلُّ
فِعْلٍ يَجْرِي عَلَى الجَوَارِحِ فَإِنَّهُ قَدْ يَرْتَفِعُ مِنْهُ أَثَرٌ إِلَى القَلْبِ.³⁹

Hence you know categorically through this that good character traits may be acquired through discipline. Deeds initially ensue from it affectedly but will eventually become second nature. This reflects the amazing relationship between the heart and the limbs – I mean between the soul and the body – because every quality

---

39. Al-Ghazālī, *Iḥyā' 'Ulūm al-Dīn*, edited by Sulaymān Dunyā, Beirut: Dār al-Maʿrifah, vol.3, p. 59.

that appears in the heart, its effect overflows to the
limbs to the extent that it will inevitably not move
except according to these effects. [The opposite is
also true;] every action of the limbs may have
an effect on the heart.

*... Indeed, Allah will not change the condition
of a people until they change what is in
themselves...* (Qur'ān 13:11)

*I*t is possible for individuals and the community to
change. There is no place in the Islamic worldview
for an 'I cannot' mentality, though Muslims and
others may fall victims to their own internal
passivity. Personal traits can be changed for the
better. When the Prophet ﷺ was chosen, at the age
of forty, to convey the universal message of Islam
to Makkah and beyond, the people of the Arabian
Peninsula had both good and bad character traits.
They were generous, truthful, courageous, but they
also fought endless tribal wars, practised infanticide,
burying their own daughters alive for fear of shame,
and drank wine. Once Islam spread, all these bad
habits were buried for good.

Islam came to endorse good behaviour. The
Prophet ﷺ said: 'Verily, I have been sent only to
perfect noble character traits'. His Companions
changed dramatically because of the Divine message
of Islam, many of them at old age. Today, those

who accept Islam may already have good moral behaviour, but they revert to the true and pure monotheistic theology. Some of them, and some born Muslims too, need to reform their characters. Imām al-Ghazālī's key concept is training which begins with the heart. Once there is a decision to mimic certain behaviour at the beginning, the limbs respond positively. One keeps repeating the exercise until the desired trait is entrenched deep in the human psyche. Performing the desired behaviour becomes easy and spontaneous.

The opposite is also true. A good person may succumb to social trends which run against divinely sanctioned personal traits, as in peer pressure, and his action may have an adverse impact on his heart. If repeated, that original good heart changes for the worse. This is when one asks: what went wrong? The community needs practical examples before its eyes. Humanity needs to examine the life of the Prophet ﷺ: *There has certainly been for you in the Messenger of Allah an excellent pattern for anyone whose hope is in Allah and the Last Day and [who] remembers Allah often.* (Qur'ān 33:21)

38

Excessive Appetite for Food Unleashes Destructive Forces

أَمَّا بَعْدُ: فَأَعْظَمُ الْمُهْلِكَاتِ لِابْنِ آدَمَ شَهْوَةُ الْبَطْنِ، فَبِهَا أُخْرِجَ
آدَمُ عَلَيْهِ السَّلَامُ وَحَوَّاءُ مِنْ دَارِ الْقَرَارِ إِلَى دَارِ الذُّلِّ وَالِافْتِقَارِ،
إِذْ نُهِيَا عَنِ الشَّجَرَةِ فَغَلَبَتْهُمَا شَهْوَاتُهُمَا حَتَّى أَكَلَا مِنْهَا فَبَدَتْ
لَهُمَا سَوْآتُهُمَا. وَالْبَطْنُ عَلَى التَّحْقِيقِ يَنْبُوعُ الشَّهَوَاتِ وَمَنْبَتُ
الْأَدْوَاءِ وَالْآفَاتِ، إِذْ يَتْبَعُهَا شَهْوَةُ الْفَرْجِ وَشِدَّةُ الشَّبَقِ إِلَى
الْمَنْكُوحَاتِ؛ ثُمَّ تَتْبَعُ شَهْوَةَ الطَّعَامِ وَالنِّكَاحِ شِدَّةُ الرَّغْبَةِ فِي
الْجَاهِ وَالْمَالِ اللَّذَيْنِ هُمَا وَسِيلَةٌ إِلَى التَّوَسُّعِ فِي الْمَنْكُوحَاتِ
وَالْمَطْعُومَاتِ؛ ثُمَّ يَتْبَعُ استِكْثَارَ الْمَالِ وَالْجَاهِ أَنْوَاعُ الرُّعُونَاتِ
وَضُرُوبُ الْمُنَافَسَاتِ وَالْمُحَاسَدَاتِ؛ ثُمَّ يَتَوَلَّدُ بَيْنَهُمَا آفَةُ الرِّيَاءِ
وَغَائِلَةُ التَّفَاخُرِ وَالتَّكَاثُرِ وَالْكِبْرِيَاءِ، ثُمَّ يَتَدَاعَى ذَلِكَ إِلَى الْحِقْدِ

وَالْحَسَدِ وَالْعَدَاوَةِ وَالْبَغْضَاءِ، ثُمَّ يُفْضِي ذَلِكَ بِصَاحِبِهِ إِلَى
اِقْتِحَامِ الْبَغْيِ وَالْمُنْكَرِ وَالْفَحْشَاءِ، وَكُلُّ ذَلِكَ ثَمَرَةُ إِهْمَالِ
الْمَعِدَةِ وَمَا يَتَوَلَّدُ مِنْهَا مِنْ بَطَرِ الشَّبَعِ وَالِامْتِلَاءِ، وَلَوْ ذَلَّلَ الْعَبْدُ
نَفْسَهُ بِالْجُوعِ وَضَيَّقَ بِهِ مَجَارِي الشَّيْطَانِ لَأَذْعَنَتْ لِطَاعَةِ
اللّٰهِ عَزَّ وَجَلَّ وَلَمْ تَسْلُكْ سَبِيلَ الْبَطَرِ وَالطُّغْيَانِ، وَلَمْ يَنْجُرَّ بِهِ
ذَلِكَ إِلَى الِانْهِمَاكِ فِي الدُّنْيَا وَإِيثَارِ الْعَاجِلَةِ عَلَى الْعُقْبَى وَلَمْ
يَتَكَالَبْ كُلُّ هَذَا التَّكَالُبِ عَلَى الدُّنْيَا. [40]

The greatest destructive source for the human being
is the appetite of the belly; it was the reason for the
expulsion of Adam ☙ and Eve from the abode of
eternal comfort to the abode of humiliation and
impoverish-ment. They were prohibited from eating
from the tree but their lust overcame them, they ate
from it and their private parts become manifest as a
result. The belly is certainly the spring of lusts and
a fertile ground for diseases and calamities. For it is
followed by the lust for sex and extreme longing for
copulation. The desire for food and sex is then followed
by extreme aspiration for status and wealth, which are
means for more food and sex. Excessive wealth and
status are then followed by different kinds of frivolous
behaviour and various forms of rivalries and resentful
envies towards others. Then between them is born the
defect of showing off, boasting and arrogance. This in
turn leads to grudges, resentful envy, animosity and
hatred. These will then prompt the person to engage in

---

40. Al-Ghazālī, *Ihyā' 'Ulūm al-Dīn*, edited by Sulaymān Dunyā,
Beirut: Dār al-Ma'rifah, vol. 3, p. 80.

oppression, wrongdoing and immorality, all of which are the results of letting the belly have its own way and what is generated of it in terms of the overbearingness of satiation and being full. Had the servant of Allah abased himself through hunger and narrowed Satan's channels, his self would have submitted to the obedience of Allah Most High, and would have neither taken the route of insolence and aggression nor would it have been dragged to immersion in this world, preferring this fleeting and immediate world over the life to come, being utterly avid for this world.

*A*nimals eat to survive. Human beings, in addition to eating to live, eat to socialise or relieve stress, as there is compulsive eating, all of which lead to physical and psychological health problems. Imām al-Ghazālī is right, the appetite for food may be destructive if it becomes out of control. He starts by referring to how human history began with eating from the Forbidden Tree. Adam and Eve could have enjoyed eating in the Garden for eternity if it were not for consuming what they should not have consumed. Transgression is what had removed them from their state of felicity.

Excessive and compulsive behaviour in food consumption leads to diseases and other problems, including an increased libido. Lust for food and sex may lead to seeking power and money to satisfy these two desires. Negative competition for money and status will ensue, and bad conduct will follow, including boastful behaviour, which is an egotistic problem. Egotism leads to negative feelings and emotions, including resentful envy, hatred and animosity. And these in turn will manifest themselves in the form of real conflicts, the hallmark of injustice, crime and sin.

When Imām al-Ghazālī advocates narrowing the channels or pathways of Satan, he is drawing on the Prophetic Sunnah. The *ḥadīth* literature shows that the worst receptacle ever filled by any human being is his belly. The Prophetic ideal of maximum eating, if one has to, is one third for food, one third for water and one third air, so that one can breathe.

The Prophet ﷺ ate in moderation, when food was available, but would subsist for a long time on water and dates as his main staple. In another tradition, the Prophet ﷺ said: 'O young men! Whoever can afford to get married should do so. And whoever cannot do so should fast, for that is his protection [against fornication].'

Allah invites us to enjoy lawful food and drink, and to be clean and adorn ourselves, especially when visiting mosques: *O children of Adam, take your adornment at every masjid, and eat and drink, but be not excessive. Indeed, He likes not those who commit excess.* (Qur'ān 7:31)

39

Healing the Love for Status

اِعْلَمْ أَنَّ مَنْ غَلَبَ عَلَى قَلْبِهِ حُبُّ الجَاهِ صَارَ مَقْصُورَ الهَمِّ عَلَى

مُرَاعَاةِ الخَلْقِ مَشْغُوفاً بِالتَوَدُّدِ إِلَيْهِمْ وَالمُرَاءاتِ لِأَجْلِهِمْ،

وَلَا يَزَالُ فِي أَقْوَالِهِ وَأَفْعَالِهِ مُلْتَفِتاً إِلَى مُعَظِّمِ مَنْزِلَتِهِ عِنْدَهُمْ وَذَلِكَ

بَذْرُ النِّفَاقِ وَأَصْلُ الفَسَادِ، وَيَجُرُّ ذَلِكَ لَا مَحَالَةَ إِلَى التَّسَاهُلِ

فِي العِبَادَاتِ وَالمُرَاءاةِ بِهَا وَإِلَى اقْتِحَامِ المَحْظُورَاتِ لِلتَوَصُّلِ

إِلَى اقْتِنَاصِ القُلُوبِ. وَلِذَلِكَ شَبَّهَ رَسُولُ اللهِ صَلَّى اللهُ عَلَيْهِ وَسَلَّمَ

حُبَّ الشَّرَفِ وَالمَالِ وَإِفْسَادِهِمَا لِلدِّينِ بِذِئْبَيْنِ ضَارِيَيْنِ.[41]

Know that the person whose heart is overcome by the love of status becomes solely preoccupied with showing deference to people, obsessed as he is with gaining favour with them and being ready to show off for their sake.

---

41. Al-Ghazālī, *Iḥyā' ʿUlūm al-Dīn*, edited by Sulaymān Dunyā, Beirut: Dār al-Maʿrifah, vol. 3, p. 287.

His only consideration in his sayings and deeds is aggrandising his standing amongst them, and this is the seed of hypocrisy and the root cause of corruption. This will inevitably lead to his negligence of the acts of worship, showing off in them and indulging in prohibited acts in order to win people's hearts. It is for this reason that the Prophet ﷺ likened the love of status and wealth and their corruption of religion to two ferocious wolves.

One of the most detrimental characteristics of human behaviour is seeking status at the expense of a principled life. Many people are willing to perform in public acts that are morally questionable in exchange for notoriety, fame and position. If it were decadent to engage in such behaviour at the time of al-Ghazālī, what would be the case in the age of social media where one may promote oneself in ways that do not please Allah?

Hunger for status may entail being hypocritical and seeking the approval of people who are believed to hold the keys to such status. This is a false sense of achievement that chips away at one's good deeds. In fact, the Prophetic tradition considers obsession with money and status worse than two hungry wolves that are allowed into a herd of sheep. They may not eat all the sheep, but they may very well kill all of them. Someone who is keen to obtain money and status at any cost runs a grave risk of bringing about the destruction of his own faith.

Trying to please everyone for the sake of material gain will lead to hypocrisy, the cornerstone of the death of truth, constructive criticism and accountability. Hypocrites have a sweet beautiful appearance and an ugly interior. Imām al-Ghazālī said that if someone greets you and asks you, 'How are you?' but does not really care about you, then he has lied to you, because he has left you with the impression that he cares about you. 'The hypocrite has three signs: when he speaks he lies; when he promises he does not keep his promise; and when he is entrusted [with something] he betrays the trust.' (Bukhārī and Muslim)

The hypocrites are mentioned in the Holy Qur'ān in many verses, and in certain contexts more than the non-believers, probably because the latter are known and their position is known to the Muslim community. The following verse shows that the hypocrite lives in constant fear of being exposed: *The hypocrites are apprehensive lest a surah be revealed about them, informing them of what is in their hearts. Say, 'Mock [as you wish]; indeed, Allah will expose that which you fear.'* (Qur'ān 9:64)

40

Revolting Against Powerful Unjust Rulers

...السُّلْطَانُ الظَّالِمُ الجَاهِلُ مَهْمَا سَاعَدَتْهُ الشَّوْكَةُ وَعَسُرَ خَلْعُهُ
وَكَانَ في الِاسْتِبْدَالِ بِهِ فِتْنَةٌ ثَائِرَةٌ لَا تُطَاقُ، وَجَبَ تَرْكُهُ
وَوَجَبَتِ الطَّاعَةُ لَهُ كَمَا تَجِبُ طَاعَةُ الأُمَرَاءِ.[42]

Even with an oppressive and ignorant ruler, as long
as he maintains military might, and it is difficult to
overthrow his power, and substituting him will lead
to a great revolt with unbearable consequences, it is
obligatory to continue obeying him just as it is
obligatory to obey legitimate leaders.

*I*mām al-Ghazālī was concerned about the bloodshed
that may accompany impeaching and removing

---

42. Al-Ghazālī, *Iḥyāʾ ʿUlūm al-Dīn*, edited by Sulaymān Dunyā,
Beirut: Dār al-Maʿrifah, vol. 2, p. 140.

dictators. This has been the predominant position among Muslim scholars who preferred maintaining the status quo rather than allowing mayhem and atrocities in society. In such a case, Muslim jurists tolerated every form of government to maintain peace and order. Preservation of life ranks high in *maqāṣid al-sharīʿah*, the main objectives of the Sacred Law. It reflects Islam's protection of life in the Holy Qurʾān and the Prophetic traditions. It is not an endorsement of dictators; it is a matter of giving people one's sympathy and support and protecting them against the wrath of those despots and their willingness to use their readily available tools of death and destruction. One has witnessed in modern times horrific attacks on civilians in more than one country in the Middle East.

In fact, unleashing the full power of the state against its own citizens will inevitably compromise all the major five objectives of Islamic Law: the protection of religion, life, intellect, property and progeny. One can also add the destruction of the environment. One may think of the role of scholars, intellectuals and activists during trying times, which might be reflected in the following Prophetic tradition: 'The greatest form of jihad is a word advocating justice before an unjust ruler.' There is a maxim in Islamic jurisprudence that says: 'Removing a specific harm should not lead to a greater harm.' The 'unbearable consequences' that Imām al-Ghazālī referred to correspond to the 'greater harm' in the above maxim; both of which should be avoided.

One has to ask deeper questions instead of always asking whether or not it is legitimate to remove dictators by using force. Questions such as: 'what can we do as a Muslim community to educate people so that we have healthy public debates with respect for rule of law and freedom of expression?' 'How can we create a constructive dialogue in the public sphere without fear of punishment?' The ruler should be aware, more than anyone else, about the Divine reward for good governance, and for his accountability and potential punishment if he resorts to despotic measures. He should remember that he is mortal and that his time on this earth will come to a term sooner or later.

References

Ghazālī, Abū Ḥāmid al-: *al-Kashf wa al-Tabyīn fī Ghurūr al-Khalq Ajmaʿīn* [*Aṣnāf al-Maghrūrīn*]. Edited by ʿAbd al-Laṭīf ʿĀshūr, Cairo: Maktabat al-Qurʾān.

———: *al-Munqidh Min al-Ḍalāl*. Edited by Jamīl Ṣalībā and Kāmil ʿAyyād, Dār al-Andalus, 1981.

———: *Bidāyat al-Hidāyah*.

———: *Tahāfut al-Falāsifah*. Edited by Sulaymān Dunyā, Cairo: Dar al-Maʿārif, 1972.

———: *Kīmiyāʾ al-Saʿādah*. Edited by Muḥammad ʿAbd al-ʿAlīm, Cairo: Maktabat al-Qurʾān.

———: *Majmūʿat Rasāʾil al-Imām al-Ghazālī*. Beirut: Dār al-Kutub al-ʿIlmiyyah, 1986.

———: *Mīzān al-ʿAmal*. Edited by Sulaymān Dunyā, Cairo: Dār al-Maʿārif, 1964.

———: *Iḥyāʾ ʿUlūm al-Dīn*. Edited by Sulaymān Dunyā, Beirut: Dār al-Maʿrifah.

Index

A

'Abd al-Raḥmān ibn 'Awf, 8

Abstention, 60

Accidents, 28

Action, 13, 20, 21, 30, 31, 34, 38, 43, 44, 48, 52, 54, 58, 60, 78, 79, 82, 88, 89, 90, 92, 93, 104, 105, 119, 131, 133, 134

Acts of worship, 119

Adam, 61, 123, 136, 137; son of, 22; children of, 61, 131, 138

Addiction(s), 24, 68

Alcohol (ism), 24, 68

Alqueria de Rosales, 5

Angels, 104; Arch, 83

Animal(s), 23, 30, 31, 41, 54

Annihilation (*fanā'*), 11

Al-Aqsa, 5, 18, 48

Arabian Peninsula, 133

Arrogance, 136

Asceticism, 75, 76

Ashʿarite, 4

Assent, 107, 108

Attachments , 16, 17, 59, 120, 122, 123

Attractions, 1, 4

Āyāt, 109

Ayyuhā al-Walad, 7

B

Backbiting, 20, 64, 65, 89, 111, 119

Baghdad, 1, 2, 17, 49

Behaviour, 8, 20, 40, 41, 52, 55, 57, 58, 59, 73, 93, 101, 104, 124, 127, 133, 134, 136, 137, 138, 140

Belief(s), 3, 28, 107, 131

Belly, 118, 136, 137, 138

Bidāyat al-Hidāyah, 9, 10

Binge drinking, 101

Boasting, 9, 73, 136

Bodily: resurrection, 28; pleasure, 68

Body, 30, 103, 114, 124, 132

Bridge-over-Hell, 40

Al-Bukhārī, 38, 141

Business, 9

C

Cambridge Muslim College, 5

Capital, 57, 38

Cell phones, 115

Children, 2, 61, 72, 73, 80, 96, 106, 107, 108, 123, 131, 138
Cleansing, 11, 59, 73, 93, 110, 111, 129
Clergy, 96
Colonisation, 79
Community, 8, 31, 37, 55, 65, 80, 105, 108, 119, 133, 141, 144
Companion(s), 8, 45, 61, 90, 124, 133
Competition, 10, 73, 137
Concentration, 115
Created beings, 55, 81, 129
Creation, 18, 31, 85, 89
Creator, 31, 54, 59, 76, 82, 130
Crime(s), 40, 110, 138
Cursing, 61, 111

𝒟

Damascus, 2, 17
Danger, 47, 89, 123
David, 126
Day of Judgment, 28, 31, 40, 41, 54, 71, 118
Death, 4, 11, 15, 82, 98, 99, 100, 101, 123, 141, 143
Delusion, 20, 72, 73, 99
Demonstration, 107
Depression, 101
Desire(s), 1, 9, 10, 12, 18, 34, 51, 64, 65, 75, 76, 103, 118, 134, 136, 137
Detachment, 17, 76, 123
Deviant theological trends, 26

Devotion, 55, 126, 131
Discomfort, 47
Disobedience(s), 20, 64, 89, 122
Distraction(s), 17, 52, 59, 101, 113, 115
Divine Will, 40, 44, 131
Dome of the Rock, 18
Drug(s), 24, 68, 101

ℰ

Eating, 13, 30, 31, 61, 115, 118, 119, 123, 136, 137, 138; over, 31, 32, 101
Economic activity, 41
Economy, 105
Education, 2, 6, 55, 104, 105, 107, 108
Egotism, 10, 11, 138
Elmhurst College, 5
Emotions, 52, 138
Enjoining good, 53, 54, 55, 56
Epic of Gilgamesh the, 100
Eternity of the world, 28
Ethics, 4, 48, 108, 126
Eve, 61, 123, 136, 137
Evil, 7, 21, 27, 40, 53, 54, 55, 56, 62
Expulsion, 61, 122, 123, 136

ℱ

Faith, 38, 43, 55, 71, 85, 89, 106, 107, 108, 111, 114, 140
False witness, 111, 112

Fame, 1, 2, 7, 8, 11, 17, 18, 49, 105, 140

Family, 2, 37, 104, 123

Fasting, 34, 90, 117, 118, 119

Fatwa, 39

Favouritism, 38

Feelings, 64, 93, 112, 115, 138

Felicity, 12, 17, 22, 23, 37, 69, 103, 104, 130, 137

Fiqh, 3, 18

Food, 13, 30, 31, 32, 41, 104, 135, 136, 137, 138

Forbidden Tree, 61, 123, 137

Forbidding evil, 53, 54, 55, 56

Forgiveness, 12, 20, 62, 71, 73, 79, 80, 93

Forms, 22, 24, 118, 130, 136

Fornication, 35, 138

Freedom, 119, 131, 144

Friends of Allah, 39, 120

Fruit(s), 42, 43, 44, 57, 58, 85, 92, 104, 105

G

Gabriel Archangel, 38, 83

Gambling, 24, 40, 41

Ghazi, 86

Glorification, 20

Gnostic, 99, 100

Gold, 11, 102, 103, 104, 105

Good (the), 13, 21, 31, 44, 59, 73, 131

Gospel, 126

Grace, 67, 68, 69

Greek, 24; metaphysics, 25, 27; philosophy, 26

H

Habits, 20, 56, 64, 65, 133

Ḥadīth, 38, 87n, 100, 111, 138

Harmony, 34

Heart(s), 2, 3, 4, 5, 8, 11, 14, 17, 18, 23, 24, 26, 34, 49, 51, 54, 57, 58, 59, 60, 71, 72, 73, 78, 79, 89, 92, 93, 95, 99, 105, 107, 110, 112, 114, 118, 119, 120, 122, 124, 125, 126, 127, 128, 129, 130, 131, 132, 133, 134, 139, 140, 141

Heaven(s), 29, 75, 82, 105, 123

Hebron, 2

Heedlessness, 114

Hereafter (Afterlife), 4, 7, 10, 16, 24, 30, 37, 40, 41, 43, 45, 67, 68, 69, 70, 71, 73, 87, 89, 95, 96, 97, 100, 101, 103, 104, 105, 108, 118, 123, 124, 127, 129

Highest Plenum, 104

History, 1, 7, 26, 59, 123, 126, 137

Hoarding, 68, 104, 105

Hope, 5, 71, 72, 82, 114, 134

Humanity, 1, 5, 8, 24, 31, 37, 49, 58, 73, 100, 123, 126, 134
Humiliation, 12, 136
Hygiene, 111

I

Idol(s), 11, 48, 83
Iḥsān, 37, 38
Illiteracy, 8
Īmān, 38
Imitation, 95, 96, 101, 107, 108
Immoral(ity), 73, 137
Impure, 71, 89; ities, 11, 93, 110, 111, 112
Inclination, 43, 92
Incoherence, 26
Income, 7, 40, 41, 114
Injustice, 37, 38, 58, 124, 138
Intellect, 5, 26, 125, 126, 127, 131, 143
Intention(s), 6, 9, 11, 16, 17, 20, 31, 40, 59, 62, 78, 89, 90, 93, 112, 119
Introspection, 16
Islām, 38
Islamic norms, 41
Islamophobes, 48
Ithāf al-Sādah al-Muttaqīn, 1

J

Jawāhir al-Qur'ān, 5
Jerusalem, 2, 18, 48
Jesus Christ, 41, 83, 126

Jokes, 65
Jugular vein, 75
Jurisprudence, 2, 3, 4, 118, 143
Justice, 36, 37, 38, 143; in, 58, 124, 138

K

Kaʿbah, 14
Karrāmiyyah, 26, 27
Khorasan, 1
Khumūl, 18
Knowledge, 1, 3, 4,6, 7, 9, 11, 24, 27, 30, 43, 48, 49, 54, 55, 58, 64, 69, 75, 78, 79, 88, 89, 90, 92, 95, 96, 102, 103, 104, 105, 109, 111, 130

L

Law(s), 3, 7, 11, 27, 34, 41, 44, 55, 119, 143, 144; ful, 40, 97, 138; Islamic, 3, 11, 41, 143; Mosaic, 41; Sacred, 7, 34, 143
Lawful meat (ḥalāl), 141
Lie(s), 22, 115, 141; Lying, 64, 65, 112
Life, 1, 3, 10, 14, 15, 23, 24, 30, 31, 34, 40, 41, 47, 48, 52, 59, 61, 68, 69, 73, 78, 79, 82, 86, 90, 95, 96, 97, 99, 100, 101, 104, 105, 108, 118, 119, 124, 127, 130, 131, 134, 137, 140, 143

Limb(s), 22, 57, 58, 59, 93, 110, 111, 118, 119, 129, 130, 131, 132, 133, 134
Logic, 26, 93, 96
Lordship, 64
Love(s), 42, 43, 44, 45, 51, 52, 58, 59, 61, 75, 76, 79, 84, 85, 86, 87, 99, 101, 130, 139, 140
Loyalty, 60, 79
Lust(s), 34, 40, 51, 64, 75, 76, 99, 136, 137

M

Madīnah, 2, 48
Main Objectives of the Sacred Law, 34, 143
Makkah, 2, 14, 48, 89, 114, 133
Manner(s), 31, 43, 57, 58
Maqāṣid al-Falāsifah, 4, 25n, 26n
Marriage, 33, 34
Marshlands, 72
Material world, 1
Mathematics, 27
Mediterranean, 47
Melody, 52
Memorisation, 107
Mercy, 34, 35, 37, 61, 130
Messenger(s), 37, 44, 61, 65, 83, 85, 86, 87, 123, 134
Metaphor, 68, 73
Metaphysics, 25, 27
Methodology, 96
Middle Ages, 2

Moderation, 69, 138
Money, 1, 8, 17, 41, 47, 49, 104, 105, 123, 137, 140
Morality, 4, 126, 137
Moral(s), 43, 55, 57, 73, 134
Mosque(s), 5, 18, 48, 115, 138
Muʿādh ibn Jabal, 66
Muʿtazilah, 26
Muḥammad (pbuh), 44, 86; The Prophet (pbuh), 7, 34, 35, 38, 40, 41, 44, 45, 48, 58, 59, 61, 66, 86, 87, 90, 100, 104, 111, 115, 124, 127, 133, 134, 138, 140
al-Munqidh min al-Ḍalāl, 1, 3, 16n, 17n
Music, 51, 101
Muslim(ṣaḥīḥ), 111, 141

N

Natural disposition (*fiṭrah*), 3, 73, 96
Negativity, 65
Neighbours, 58
Niẓāmiyyah, 1, 2, 17

O

Occasionalism, 81, 82
Oppression, 137

P

Pain, 65, 78, 80, 97, 100
Paradise, 24, 65, 66

People of the Book, 131
Perfection, 12, 75, 129
Personal: opinion, 40; taste, 40; traits, 4, 132, 133, 134
Philosophy, 2, 17n, 26
Physics, 27
Piety, 17, 30, 39, 40, 41
Pilgrimage, 14, 48, 89, 118, 119, 124
Plant(s), 71, 72, 73
Pleasure(s), 12, 13, 22, 23, 24, 48, 56, 67, 68, 69, 79, 97, 100, 103, 104
Pork, 41
Position(s), 1, 2, 6, 7, 8, 11, 17, 26, 64, 140, 141, 143
Poverty, 8, 47, 82
Power, 2, 8, 49, 137, 142, 143
Prayer(s), 18, 65, 66, 86, 89, 111, 114, 115, 116, 118, 119, 126, 130
Predecessors, 30
Pride, 19, 20, 129
Profit, 37, 38
Progeny, 34, 131, 143
Proof(s), 3, 26, 85, 107, 108
Prophetic Practice, 31
Prophets, 37, 44, 45, 54, 55, 82, 111, 112, 123
Psalms, 126
Psychology, 41, 107
Public servant, 8
Purification, 110, 111, 112

Q
Al-Quds, 5
Qur'ān, 3, 5, 19n, 22n, 24, 27, 30, 34, 35, 37, 38, 41, 43, 44, 55, 61, 62, 64, 65, 73, 75, 80, 82, 83, 86, 87, 89, 90, 92, 99, 100, 101, 105, 109, 115, 123, 125, 126, 127, 131, 133, 134, 138, 141, 143

R
Rābiʿah al-ʿAdawiyyah, 10
Ramadan, 5, 90, 119
Ratiocination, 95, 96
Reason(s), 5, 8, 27, 47, 54, 65, 66, 79, 104, 112, 114, 136, 140
Recitation, 125
Regret, 78, 99
Rejection, 59, 60, 123
Reliance, 82
Remembrance, 58, 73
Repentance, 20, 21, 60, 61, 62, 78, 79, 80, 99, 100, 122, 124
Responsibility, 8, 21, 54, 129
Revelation(s), 27, 40, 112, 123, 126
Rivalry, 9
Ruler(s), 142, 143, 144

S
Sahl ibn ʿAbdullāh al-Tustarī, 60
Salt swamps, 71

Sanitation, 8
Satan, 61, 64, 65, 93, 137, 138
Schisms, 26
Scholarship, 10
Seclusion, 34, 105
Secret(s), 58, 91, 92, 93, 110
Self-aggrandisement, 10
Servitude, 64
Sex, 33, 34, 136, 137
Sexuality, 34, 51
Shafiʿī Imām, 48; School, 4
Shortcoming(s), 75, 100, 114
Showing off, 10, 64, 89, 136, 140
Silver, 102, 103, 104, 105
Sincerity, 26, 88, 89, 90
Sin(s), 20, 35, 40, 44, 60, 61, 62, 63, 64, 65, 73, 77, 78, 79, 80, 86, 89, 110, 111, 118, 122, 124, 138; ful, 93, 111, 112
Social media, 76, 101, 140
Society, 8, 143
Song(s), 50, 51, 52
Sorrow, 15, 100
Sound(s), 22, 24, 30, 115, 126, 127, 129
Space and time, 75, 83
Spain, 5
Spiritual crisis, 1
Spirituality, 2, 3, 26, 31, 34, 90, 96, 118, 119, 126
Statues, 17, 23, 47, 90, 104, 105, 136, 137, 139, 140, 143

Stomach, 32
Struggle, 1, 59, 85
Stupidity, 72
Al-Subkī, 2
Success, 8, 37, 129
Sufi(s), 1, 4, 11, 18
Suicide, 14, 24, 52
Sunnah, 3, 27, 34, 54, 55, 56, 73, 115, 127, 138
Supplication(s), 18, 79, 89, 115, 130

T

Ṭabaqāt al-Shāfiʿiyyah al-Kubrā, 2
Tahāfut al-Falāsifah, 25n, 26n, 27
Tawḥīd, 82, 96
Teacher(s), 10, 31, 96
Temptation, 59, 61
Tenets of faith, 107
The Revival of the Religious Sciences (Iḥyāʾ ʿUlūm al-Dīn), 3, 10
Theology, 2, 27, 28, 83, 109, 126, 134
Thomas Aquinas, 4
Thought(s), 2, 34, 35, 52, 56, 57, 73, 92, 93, 105, 114, 115, 118
Toil, 12, 14, 89, 122
Tongue, 1, 2, 19, 20, 64, 65, 66, 112, 118, 119, 125, 126, 127
Torah, 41, 126
Trade, 37
Tranquillity, 34, 35, 93
Transgression, 52, 79, 137

Travel(ler), 47, 48, 119, 122, 123, 124
Travelling, 46, 47, 48, 49, 124
Trust, 82, 141
Tus, 1
TV programmes, 101

U

Ummah, 55, 85
Understanding, 3, 107, 127
Universe, 31, 59, 76, 82, 89, 92, 109, 130
ʿUthmān ibn ʿAffān, 8

V

Violence, 112

W

Wāqifiyyah, 26, 27
Watchfulness, 92
Water, 8, 49, 71, 72, 111, 138

Wealth, 1, 2, 7, 10, 11,13, 14, 17, 23, 41, 47, 68, 69, 73, 80, 82, 105, 136, 140
Wellbeing, 79, 103
Wine, 61, 133
Wishful thinking, 72
Worldview(s), 3, 24, 27, 41, 55, 79, 96, 108, 109, 127, 133
Worship, 14, 20, 23, 31, 33, 34, 38, 43, 48, 55, 58, 82, 89, 90, 118, 119, 129, 131, 140
Wrongdoing, 34, 58, 61, 93, 137

X

Xenophobia, 47

Z

al-Zabīdī, 1
Zaytuna College, 5